Knitting Outside the Box: Drape & Fold

Bristol Ivy

POM POM PRESS
LONDON

Knitting Outside the Box: Drape & Fold

Published in 2019
by Pom Pom Press

Text © 2019
Bristol Ivy

Pattern Photography © 2019
Amy Gwatkin

Swatch Photography © 2019
Carrie Bostick Hoge

ISBN:
978-1-9160295-1-4

A catalogue record for this book is available from the British Library.

Editors:
Meghan Fernandes and Lydia Gluck

Managing Editor:
Amy Collins

Artwork:
Bless Design

Media Manager:
Sophie Scott

Marketing Director:
Francesca Baldry

Studio Managers:
Gayle Taliaferro Gilner and Iesha Parker

Production Assistant:
Alice Sleight

Lead Technical Editor:
Amelia Hodsdon

Second Technical Editor:
Emma Thursby

Pattern Photography:
Amy Gwatkin

Swatch Photography:
Carrie Bostick Hoge

Illustrations:
Bristol Ivy

Copy Editor:
Annie Prime

Consultant:
Emi Ito

Model:
Nyome Nicholas Williams

Photographer's Assistant:
Tom Hall

Hair & Makeup:
Jenny Green

Photoshoot Location:
Clapton Hart, London

Jewellery Provided By:
Wolf & Moon and Melanie Eddy

Sample Knitters:
Alison Hellyer, Amy Philip, Bonnie Politano, Chaitanya Muralidhara, Chonita Olivas, Darlene Ivy, Jessica Krop, Minh Nguyen, Rebecca Yohe

Test Knitters:
Anoush Emrazian Anderson, Belle Sutton, Carol Roe, Catarina Almeida, Erendis of Numenor, Eva-Maria Treichel, Fie Bundgaard Nielsen, Grace Nye, Heather Noyes, Jacqui Zurawski, Jaimie Noy, Jen Aubrecht, Jessica Sherman, Leigh Beamer, Lynné Diaz, Sophie Scott, Sophie Thomas, Steph Gillette, Stacy Washington

For pattern corrections, please visit pompommag.com/errata

Printed in the UK by:
Pureprint Group Limited

POM POM PRESS
Hackney Downs Studios
Charcoal Hall
Amhurst Terrace
London E8 2BT
United Kingdom

Stay in Touch:
pompommag.com
ravelry.com/groups/pom-pom
instagram.com/pompommag
facebook.com/pompommag
twitter.com/pompommag
pinterest.com/pompommag

Contents

Editors' Foreword

During a quiet moment at the 2017 New York State Sheep and Wool Festival, in the midst of the whirlwind launch of the first iteration of *Knitting Outside the Box*, Bristol Ivy told us she already had ideas to follow up on the book we were only just introducing to the knitting world. Releasing a new title is exciting and nerve-wracking in equal measures, but we already knew we'd want to continue publishing her work. Almost two years later, we are so proud to be writing this foreword to the second volume.

Bristol is an unstoppable creative force and one of the most philosophical designers around. This book is as innovative and exciting as the first instalment because Bristol continues to reimagine the way we make fabric (she's still thinking outside the box!). Her interrogation of the basic principles of how and why we construct knitted clothing yields designs that are at once innovative and classic.

Along with her inventive techniques and thoughts on making, Bristol always adds a dash of humour. The curiosity, joy, generosity, and compassion she brings to our community is palpable. We hope you will share in these happy feelings and find this book as inspiring as we do. We can't wait to see the beautiful things this book helps to create.

Lydia Gluck & Meghan Fernandes
London / July 2019

Author's Foreword

This story begins with a small child's clumsy fingers, a square of construction paper, and the instructions to fold a simple paper cup. I'm sure it wasn't beautiful and I'm sure it wasn't remotely noteworthy on the list of day-to-day activities my mother kept as she homeschooled me in the Waldorf tradition (which holds that crafts such as paper folding encouraged creative thinking,) but my four-year-old self was entranced. I was captivated by the idea that a flat piece of paper could fold into a three-dimensional object to make something that was useful and could even hold water. It was a seminal moment in how my brain processed the world around me. 2D could become 3D, 3D could become 2D (as I learned when I accidentally squished the cup flat), and the universe of visual perception and manipulation was mine to play with.

These themes popped up again and again throughout my life, from a fascination with paper folding and origami, to experiments in fabric manipulation and drape (thanks partly to my mom's stash of quilting fabric and some scissors she probably didn't plan on me finding). As a teenager with a newfound passion for fashion, the pages of magazines I would obsess over the most were those that took clothing in a different direction with unusual construction, using unexpected curves, twists, pleats, and billows of fabric to accentuate and flatter the human body. The structures and unexpected shaping of Cristóbal Balenciaga, Elsa Schiaparelli, and Madeleine Vionnet's fluid, mesmerically draped dresses were often made of a single piece of fabric clipped in just a few places and draped into a startlingly modern form. The pleats and gathers of Madame Grès and Issey Miyake created volume, unexpected folds, and non-traditional garment shapes. Junya Watanabe combined expected fabrics with unexpected proportions. Even the more classic femininity and vintage decadence of Christian Dior's New Look relied on an innovative approach to draping that added another dimension with surprising construction techniques. These designers captured both my heart and my brain. While I loved (and still love) all clothing as an expression of art and joy, the designers who seemed to ask 'what if?' made clothing that, to me, felt like home.

I kept coming back to these ideas when I started to explore knitting design. As I said in *Knitting Outside the Box*, the first book in this series: just because something has usually been done a certain way in the past doesn't mean it must continue to be done that way. This is true in how knitted fabric is constructed, but also in the structure of the garment itself. Raglans, set-in sleeves, yokes—this is how sweaters have been made in the past.

But, as my fingers knit away on these shapes, my brain went back to that paper folding as a kid and those images in the magazines as a teenager, and I realised how these techniques might fit into this new world of mine. I came to understand that knitters have the skills to design the structure and composition of the fabric itself, yes, but we can also take that next step: we can explore what happens to the fabric after it's created. We have the ability (even the permission!) to treat our knitting not just as set shapes that can be filled with whatever stitch patterns we want or from whatever direction we want. We also have the ability to change those shapes and to create brand-new silhouettes and outlines by manipulating the fabric itself using draping and folds.

I have continued playing with this concept throughout my career as a knitting designer. I still use paper and fabric forms to develop pattern ideas. In this book, I want to share some ways I've found to manipulate knitted fabric after its creation. This is by no means a complete list, but it is a place from which to start pushing the boundaries of what we consider possible with knitting.

Bristol Ivy
Portland, Maine / July 2019

A Note on Pattern Naming and Diagrams

In the original *Knitting Outside the Box*, I named the patterns after strong women who made huge strides in their occupations and vocations. Here, I continue this practice—with a nod to my own history with drape and fold—by naming these patterns after origami artists and fashion designers who pushed the boundaries of construction and design process.

Paper folding has multiple international traditions but the current art form is by far most indebted to Japanese origami. Throughout the folding diagrams in this book, I have used the Yoshizawa-Randlett system, devised by Akira Yoshizawa in the 1950s and 1960s to provide simple origami instructions. It is the clearest diagramming system I know and has become the international standard for the art of paper folding. Though my designs are not origami, I hope that the use of this diagramming system will honour the artists who have made folding the inspiring and deeply meaningful art form that it is today.

As a way to give back to the culture that created this diagramming method and shaped some of my ideas about folding, and because the treatment and experience of Japanese Americans in the United States is historically fraught, Pom Pom Press and I have decided to donate 5% of the proceeds of each book sale to Denshō, in hopes of honouring the Japanese-heritage people named in these pages. Denshō is an organisation that seeks to chronicle, preserve, and disseminate information about the incarceration of Japanese Americans during World War II. They do valuable work to make sure we do not forget what we are capable of as humans, both in atrocity on the one hand, and in hope, resistance, and resilience on the other.

To learn more about the incarceration of Japanese Americans, please visit densho.org.

Introduction

This slim volume comprises the next chapter of the *Knitting Outside the Box* saga. We're going to do things a little differently from now on; think of these as addenda, as ways to continue stretching the boundaries of what we consider knitting to be.

In the previous volume of *Knitting Outside the Box*, I focused on the way we can shape fabric from the inside out, how we can manipulate and manifest a garment from its very bones outward. Like I've said before (and I'll likely say until the day I die), knitting has traditions, *but knitting doesn't have rules*. We can create our fabric any way we want to, from any direction, to any finished form we like. We can let the shape dictate the technique, asking our stitches to conform to the proportions of a specific outline, mixing techniques and skills to get exactly what we want. Or we can let the technique dictate the shape, asking 'what if?' and letting the structure of the fabric tell us how it wants to end up. With both of these as guiding principles, I discussed increasing and decreasing, short rows, and stitch patterns that manipulate your gauge as ways to shape your fabric itself from the ground up. One thing I didn't talk about, however, was another possible step after the fabric is complete. You can use all these things to manipulate the fabric as you make it, true, but it's also possible to manipulate the fabric *once it comes off the needles*.

This book takes that next step and focuses on the fundamental concepts of drape and folding. Knitting is the creation of a piece of fabric that, 95% of the time, exists on a flat plane. However, human bodies are not flat planes. We have bumps and curves, changes in angle, places where fabric clings and places where fabric falls gracefully away. And if knitting weren't flexible in accommodating these, we'd all be walking around in the sartorial equivalent of cardboard boxes.

Therefore, any time we knit a garment, we do so under the subconscious understanding that, no matter what, those flat planes—those fundamentally columnar and row-based bits of geometry that knitting creates—will drape, fold, twist, bend, and conform to our shape.

When we think about drape and folding in the larger knitting picture, we start seeing the referents everywhere. What is a cardigan but a flat piece of fabric that bends and folds around the body to meet in the front? What is a scarf but a long thin shape that we wrap and wrap around ourselves into a cylinder (albeit one without tethers to keep it in place)? And a sock must fold at the heel (whether through short row or heel flap) to accommodate the flex and change in direction of the transition between the ankle and the foot. We already unthinkingly accommodate our 3D reality into our 2D knitting. Why not take it one step further?

In most typical garment construction, seams are the answer to natural changes in angle and direction on a human body. They help us break down the 3D form of a human body into smaller, 2D chunks: sweater fronts and sweater backs, for example, change direction and angle at the shoulder and side seams. In addition, sleeves change direction at the armscye. This is a valid and useful method of construction, one that I've used in this very book! However, we can also hinge the fabric itself at those locations, *wrapping* around those changes in angle and shifts in direction to create a much softer, smoother line.

Let's go back to the placement of seams in typically-constructed garments. Usually, as we approach the front shoulder of a sweater, we would work stepped cast-offs or short-row shaping to have the edge of our piece mimic the slope of the shoulder.

What would happen if instead we continued working the piece straight, and folded it over the angle of the shoulder? This angle of the shoulder would change the direction of the fabric, sending it towards the centre back to meet its twin from the other front shoulder instead. You could then pick up and knit down from the centre point of the chevron to create the back, or seam a back piece to those front bars, or work a chevron down from there... the possibilities are limitless. Working with this one small fold in our garment opens up the possibilities of non-traditional construction, a shape more organically fitted to the body's curves and bends, and a place to play with pattern and structure in a way traditional formats don't allow.

You can also use folding and drape in knitwear to move beyond these traditional garment structures. To me, a garment is a basic outline, and you can fill in that outline with knitting from any direction and with any stitch pattern you like. But one of my big revelations while working on this book was that knitwear can be classified entirely by the number of holes for heads, torsos, appendages, and digits a garment has. I'm half-joking, but it holds relatively true (unless you talk to topological mathematicians, but that's a topic for later conversation):

- Zero holes: a shawl or scarf.
  You wrap these around you and, unless knotted or pinned, they remain unsecured and unanchored by a defined hole for your head.

- One hole: a hat.
  You need the hole on the bottom of the hat for your head to go into.

- Two holes: a cowl.
  One hole for your head to go into and one hole for your head to come out of.

- Three holes: a cardigan.
  One hole each for your arms, and one large opening for your head and your torso, the front opening of the cardigan.

- Four holes: a pullover.
  One hole each for your arms, one hole for your head, and one hole for your torso.

Other garments fit in with a bit of tweaking: socks are long one-holes with a bend in the middle. Mittens are one-holes with a smaller one-hole on the side. It sounds silly, but it's a useful perspective, and it opens up the possibilities for what a garment can be. The garments in this book aren't traditional constructions or traditional shapes. As such I've done some thoughtful and preservational things (stabilising seams, three-needle cast-offs, fabric on the bias) to help ensure that the drapiness and construction of the fabric won't overwhelm the garment or pull it out of shape. But if these garments have the right number of holes, if they have these stabilising details to keep them in shape, if they expand the boundaries of how we think about construction, and if they make you feel beautiful, then... why not? As I said in the first volume of *Knitting Outside the Box*, just because something is the common paradigm doesn't mean it's the only paradigm.

We are capable of so much more in knitting, bringing it into a new world of creativity and divergence. I hope this book gives you yet another tool to do so.

Foundations

While there is truly no limit to what's possible with fold and drape in fabric, there are a few major methods that form the foundation and shape all other possibilities.

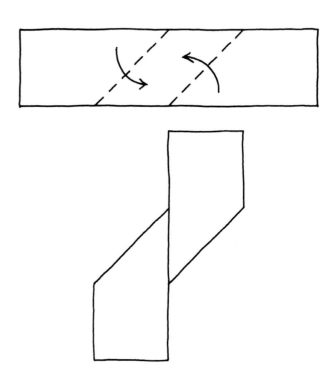

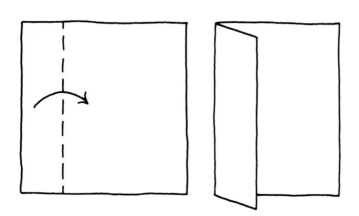

Fold

Fold is the basis for all further methods of drape. When we strip it back to the essentials, as we talked about before, every knitted garment is folded in some way. To fold in knitwear, as I am defining it here, is *to bring the edges or vertices (points) of the fabric together in such a way that they meet up, either parallel or perpendicular*. These folds can be horizontal, vertical, or diagonal—each gives a different flow and sense of movement to your finished garment. Folding can also be worked with any shape of fabric, though I tend to stick with squares and rectangles as they have clean straight edges to manipulate and they provide more than enough options to play with!

Overlap

Overlapping is a further version of folding, but in this case, it occurs *when edges, especially parallel edges, meet but the vertices of the shape don't line up*. This can be one of the most interesting forms of manipulation in knitting. We are used to edges meeting neatly and evenly at common vertices, which tends to preserve the geometric and angular shapes inherent in the linear nature of knitting. But with overlapping pieces, we take it past that common meeting point, twisting the fabric on itself or joining or spiralling it away from its original direction. Overlapping distorts the fabric from its beginning dimensions and angles, creating something far more organic and fluid. As with folding, overlapping can be worked on any shape, but again it can be helpful to stick to shapes with clean straight edges to avoid any buckling or distortion in the seaming process.

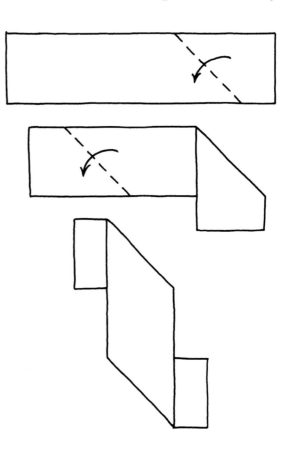

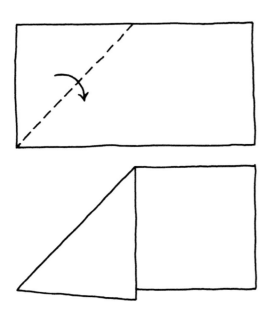

Rotate

Rotation occurs in knitting **when the fabric is seamed or joined along a perpendicular edge as opposed to a parallel one. This can be done either alone or in concert with a garment silhouette that, when laid flat, forms a far more extreme angle than that of a traditional construction.** Both of these ensure that the fabric will drop and billow when worn on a human body. These two constructions exaggerate or wildly change our expectations of a garment's silhouette, but create stunning drama and grace when worn. In the first iteration, think of a garment where the back of the sweater is knit in a traditional shape, but the front is knit as an upside-down T. If we seam the tops of the arms of the T to the sides of the normal back piece, the fabric will flex and bend into a much softer, more fluid form than the pieces would make it seem! In the second iteration, think of a whole garment shaped like an upside-down T, with armholes in the sides of the upright and a neck opening at the top of the upright. When laid flat, this piece does not bear any resemblance to a human body! But when worn, gravity pulls the arms of the T down against the body, folding and draping the fabric around the form beautifully. In both of these cases, the fabric stays flat or folds on itself slightly when laid out; it doesn't distort like overlapping fabric or turn on itself like twisting fabric.

Twist

Twist takes overlapping and rotation one step further: it is **when the fabric itself rotates, using the twist to turn a flat plane into a 3D shape.** If **overlap** brings the dimensions of the fabric into a 3D form but keeps the same side up at all times, and **rotate** maintains a flat fabric but changes and drapes when worn, twist is the middle ground between the two. This means introducing a turn into the fabric itself, twisting it 180 degrees so that both the right side and wrong side are visible at the same time (as with a Moebius strip), or turning it fully so that it makes a full 360-degree rotation and comes back to the right side again. When these twisted pieces of fabric are joined in the round or seamed together, the twists lift certain portions of the fabric off the flat plane, creating a 3D shape that wends and winds its way around the human form.

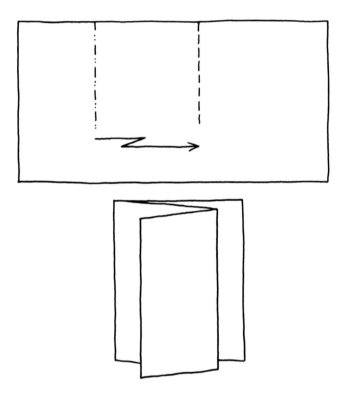

One thing you'll notice about these definitions is that the dividing lines between each are very fluid, and a lot of structures are hard to define as just one thing. But typically one or two of these techniques start the garment on its process and form the overarching aesthetic or technical motif that moves it forward. In addition, all of these techniques can be used on any shape of fabric that you desire. Some are easier than others, sure, but you can create these shapes in any way and from any direction you want. The act of folding occurs after the fabric itself is created, and therefore gives us space to be creative and thoughtful during the evolution of the fabric itself.

Furthermore, all these shapes lend themselves well to the fabric manipulation we discussed in the original *Knitting Outside the Box*. If you wanted to, you could easily use increasing or decreasing, short rows, or stitch patterns that manipulate your gauge to aid in the folding process. Perhaps at the folding point, you could work some short rows to create some shoulder shaping and secure the garment on your shoulder, or work a welt to help the fabric fold easily at that point. In that case, you have the best of both worlds: you're shaping the fabric both before and after construction for a garment that truly fits your body—and your mind!

Pleat

While all other forms of fabric manipulation that we've discussed so far typically involve opposing edges meeting, overlapping, and joining together, pleating fabric is one of the few instances in which we manipulate a single edge or section against itself only. Pleating occurs **when the same edge or portion of fabric folds onto itself**, gathering it in, creating structure, and altering the dimensions of the garment. When a piece of fabric is pleated on itself, it doubles or triples in thickness while also halving or thirding its length—a magical combination that adds stability in one part of the garment and drape in an alternate part.

Foundations
Swatches

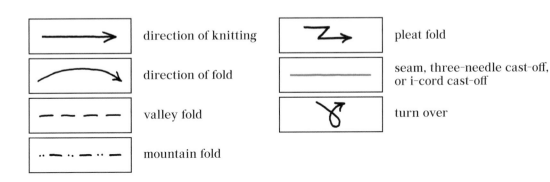

direction of knitting

direction of fold

valley fold

mountain fold

pleat fold

seam, three-needle cast-off,
or i-cord cast-off

turn over

The "Barn Roof"
Utilising Fold, Rotate

Starting with a rectangle approximately twice as wide as it is tall, this shape employs two valley *folds* to *rotate* the top points of the rectangle down towards the centre. Once they meet the bottom edge, they are seamed into place to secure the fold. The extreme angles at the edges, if knit in a stiffer fabric and/or at a smaller gauge, would ensure a dramatic and graphic oversized-poncho silhouette. If knit in a drapier fabric, the points would likely drape down to rest against the body, creating fluid swing and movement.

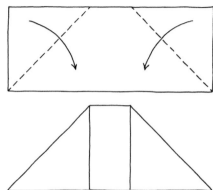

The "Map of Maine"
Utilising Rotate, Pleat

This swatch uses **pleats** on the background of a square piece of fabric to drastically reduce one edge of the square, rendering it able to **rotate** and seam to a perpendicular edge. This creates a louche and sculptural cowl, with fabric folded on the bias and a breezy bandana shape.

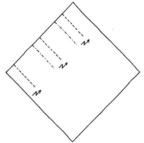
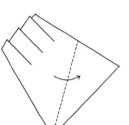

The "Opera Cloak"
Utilising Fold, Overlap

Playing with asymmetry and drama, this construction *folds* two points of this rectangular panel in to meet and partially seam each other. This leaves an opening for an armhole, and creates a gentle cocoon around half of the body with a gracefully-angled shoulder line. The remainder of the fabric is valley-folded down to *overlap* and sit perpendicular to the first seam. In doing so, this mirrors and echoes the shoulder line of the first half, but extends it down over the arm to create a dramatic shawl or cape that, due to the seams, might actually stay put!

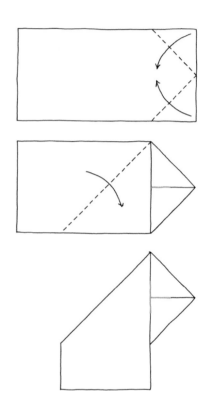

The "Meet in the Middle"
Utilising Fold

Sometimes only the barest hint of a seam is needed to create a new shape. Here, the points of this square piece of fabric are *folded* in to meet and join each other at the centre, creating a tube with extravagant points at either end. These could be the bases upon which other shapes are picked up and knit, or they could be worn as is to create drama and flair.

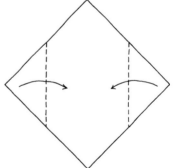

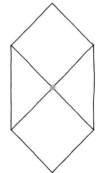

The "Superhero Cape"
Utilising Fold, Rotate, Overlap

Though employing the simplest of valley folds, this piece takes those *folds* along different angles to create two very different structures within the fabric. The right edge of the rectangular fabric is folded in parallel, and the left edge is folded on the diagonal to *rotate* the edge of the fabric perpendicularly. These are then *overlapped* and seamed together, adding stability from the fold on the grainline of the fabric and drape and fluidity from the bias fold.

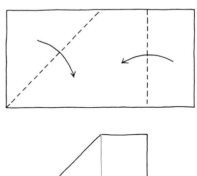

The "Reversible Hug"
Utilising Twist, Fold

The Moebius strip is a form that shows up often in knitting, and can seem intimidating at the start. But in essence, it is a combination of continual *folds* in the fabric that, when done in sequence, add a half-*twist* to the swatch and expose both the right and the wrong sides of the work. Here, the extra-long rectangle *folds* once on itself on the bias at the centre of the fabric. It then rotates so that fold becomes the bottom edge, and the sides fold back to meet in the middle and seam together to form a tube. This can be worn as is, as seen in the many Moebius patterns out there in the knitting world, or could be the basis for a further construction. What if those two angles at the bottom edge were armholes, and the V at the top a neck opening?

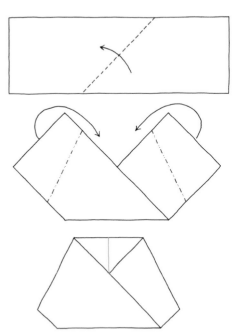

The "Strand of DNA"
Utilising Overlap, Fold, Rotate

Overlapping fabric in knitting is often where the most subversive and unexpected shapes occur. Here, this extra-long rectangle explores what might happen if we *folded*, and folded, and kept on folding… all in the same direction. This *rotates* the fabric around itself, creating an organic and surprising curlicue of fabric. When these folds are seamed into place, with the top edge seaming to the bottom edge along the whole length, it creates a long tube on the bias that could create the base for a sleeve, a body, or a cowl.

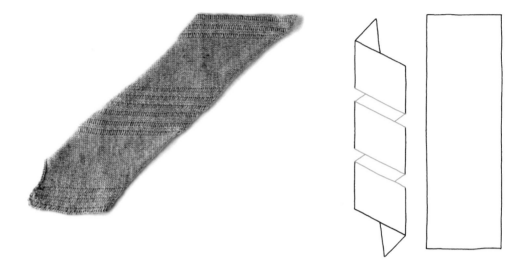

The "T-Shirt"
Utilising Pleat

Pleats are one of the best ways to mimic a body's changes in shape without increasing or decreasing the stitch count. Imagine if you have an allover cable pattern that would be a hassle to incorporate shaping into—what might happen if you pleated the fabric at the top edge as a replacement for armhole shaping? Here, two square pieces of fabric are both pleated on either side of the top edge, and joined together along the pleats and along the bottom half of each side seam.

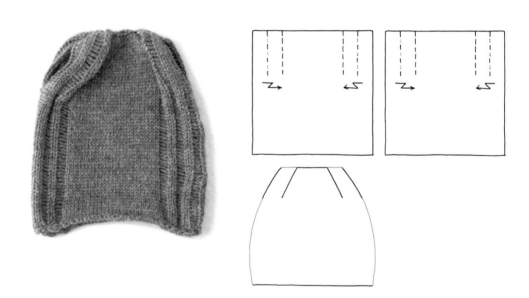

The "Ballet Dancer"
Utilising Fold

Sometimes the simplest ideas can be the best. Here, a square piece of fabric is *folded* so that the top and bottom edges meet in the middle. Seams are added at each edge, joining the ends into tubes and leaving space in the centre for a body opening. It creates a clean, sophisticated and wearable silhouette that is also the perfect canvas for stitch pattern and detail.

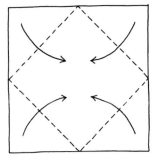

The "All Together Now"
Utilising Fold, Rotate

Starting from a square piece of fabric, this silhouette *folds* and *rotates* all four corners together into the centre to create a soft and graceful cocoon. In a typical use of this construction, seams are added at the horizontal meeting points, creating one large body opening in the centre and two smaller ones for armholes. But here, the vertical edges have been seamed as well to make a pullover, leaving an opening for the head at the top and one for the body at the bottom. Sleeves could be added, a turtleneck or shawl collar could join on to the top—all from the basis of four simple folds.

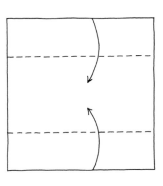

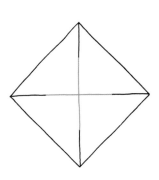

Patterns

Fold: Vionnet

Based on folding's simple principles of edges meeting around the gentle curves of the shoulders and waist, the graceful and elegant bias construction of Vionnet is enhanced by twisted cables and an oversized front collar.

Named after Madeleine Vionnet, one of the first fashion designers to cut and drape fabric on the bias to create fluid, elegant gowns that moved and stretched with the body.

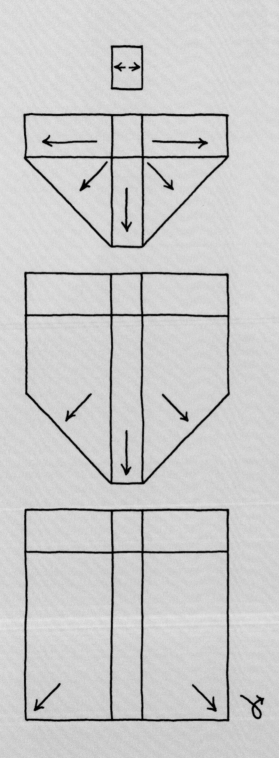

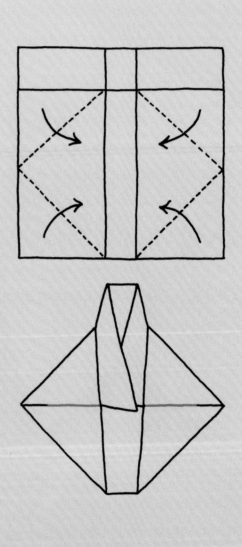

Sizes:

1 (2, 3, 4, 5, 6, 7, 8)

Finished back width:

90 (95, 98, 101, 106, 108, 111, 113)cm / 35½ (37½, 38½, 39½, 41½, 42½, 43½, 44½)" back width, to fit 76-86 (86.5-96, 96.5-106, 106.5-116, 116.5-126, 126.5-136, 136.5-146, 146.5-156)cm / 30-33 ¾ (34-37¾, 38-41¾, 42-45¾, 46-49¾, 50-53½, 54-57¾, 58-61¾)" bust circumference

Model has 127cm / 50" bust, stands 175cm / 5'9" tall, and is wearing size 5.

Yarn: Stolen Stitches (pictured p34, p35)

Nua (sport weight; 60% Merino, 20% yak, 20% linen; 140m / 153yds per 50g skein)

Shade: Kitten Fluff (9810); 11 (12, 12, 12, 13, 13, 13, 14) skeins

OR

Yarn: La Bien Aimée (pictured p27, p31)

Merino DK (DK weight; 100% superwash Merino; 230m / 252yds per 115g skein)

Shade: Direwolf; 7 (8, 8, 8, 9, 9, 9, 9) skeins

Gauge:

23 sts & 32 rows = 10cm / 4" over stocking stitch on 4mm needles after blocking.

25 sts & 31 rows = 10cm / 4" over cable pattern on 4mm needles after blocking.

18 sts & 40 rows = 10cm / 4" over twisted rib on 3.75mm needles after blocking.

Needles:

4mm / US 6 circular needle, 80cm / 32" length

3.75mm / US 5 circular needle, 150cm / 60" length, **AND** needle suitable for working small circumferences

Always use a needle size that will result in the correct gauge after blocking.

Notions:

Crochet hook and waste yarn for provisional cast-on, 3 locking stitch markers, 4 stitch holders or waste yarn, stitch markers, 2 cable needles, tapestry needle

Notes:

Vionnet is started from the centre back neck with a provisional cast-on for a garter and twisted rib square. Once this is complete, Vionnet is worked as for a top-down shawl until the body width is reached. Once there, it's worked as a chevron until the body length is reached. After that, stitches are decreased on either side to fill in the remainder of the square. Once the body is complete, the border is picked up around three edges and worked in twisted rib, and then three-needle cast-offs are worked on the side edges to create armholes.These armholes are then finished with twisted ribbing. When Right and Left parts of the garment are referred to, they are the wearer's right and left.

Stitch Glossary:

1/1 LPT: Sl 1 to cable needle, hold in front, p1, k1tbl from cable needle.
1/1 RPT: Sl 1 to cable needle, hold in back, k1tbl, p1 from cable needle.
1/2 LPT: Sl 1 to cable needle, hold in front, p2, k1tbl from cable needle.
1/2 RPT: Sl 2 to cable needle, hold in back, k1tbl, p2 from cable needle.

1/1/1 LPT: Sl 1 to cable needle, hold in front, slip next st to a second cable needle and hold in back, k1tbl, p1 from back cable needle, k1tbl from front cable needle.

TWISTED RIB
ROW 1 (RS): K1, k1tbl, [p1, k1tbl] to end.
ROW 2 (WS): [P1tbl, k1] to last 2 sts, p1tbl, p1.

SSK CAST-OFF: Ssk, *slip next st knitwise to right needle, insert left needle through front of both sts on right needle, k2togtbl; rep from * to end.

CHARTS – WRITTEN INSTRUCTIONS

CABLE PANEL

ROW 1 (RS): K1tbl, p1, [1/2 LPT, p1, k1tbl, p3, k1tbl, p1, 1/2 RPT, p1] to last st, k1tbl.
ROW 2 (WS): P1tbl, [k2, (p1tbl) twice, k1, p1tbl, k3, p1tbl, k1, (p1tbl) twice, k1] to last 2 sts, k1, p1tbl.
ROW 3: K1tbl, p1, [p1, k1tbl, 1/2 LPT, p3, 1/2 RPT, k1tbl, p2] to last st, k1tbl.
ROW 4: P1tbl, [(k2, p1tbl) twice, k3, p1tbl, k2, p1tbl, k1] to last 2 sts, k1, p1tbl.
ROW 5-8: Rep rows 1-4.
ROW 9: K1tbl, p1, [p1, k1tbl, p2, 1/1 LPT, p1, 1/1 RPT, p2, k1tbl, p2] to last st, k1tbl.
ROW 10: P1tbl, [k2, p1tbl, k3, p1tbl, k1, p1tbl, k3, p1tbl, k1] to last 2 sts, k1, p1tbl.
ROW 11: K1tbl, p1, [p1, k1tbl, p3, 1/1/1 LPT, p3, k1tbl, p2] to last st, k1tbl.
ROW 12: Rep row 10.
ROW 13: K1tbl, p1, [p1, k1tbl, p2, 1/1 RPT, p1, 1/1 LPT, p2, k1tbl, p2] to last st, k1tbl.
ROW 14: Rep row 8.
ROW 15: K1tbl, p1, [p1, k1tbl, 1/2 RPT, p3, 1/2 LPT, k1tbl, p2] to last st, k1tbl.
ROW 16: Rep row 2.
ROW 17: K1tbl, p1, [1/2 RPT, p1, k1tbl, p3, k1tbl, p1, 1/2 LPT, p1] to last st, k1tbl.
ROW 18: Rep row 4.
ROWS 19-21: Rep rows 15-17.
ROW 22: P1tbl, [k1, p1tbl, (k3, p1tbl) 3 times] to last 2 sts, k1, p1tbl.
ROW 23: 1/1/1 LPT, [(p3, k1tbl) twice, p3, 1/1/1 LPT] to end.
ROW 24: Rep row 22.

PATTERN BEGINS

RIGHT BACK NECK TAB

Using the larger circular needle, and a provisional method, provisionally cast on 60 sts. Do not join.

Work 6 rows in garter st (knit every row).
SET-UP ROW (WS): [P1tbl, k1] to last 2 sts, p1tbl, p1.
ROW 1 (RS): K1, k1tbl, [p1, k1tbl] to end.
ROW 2: [P1tbl, k1] to last 2 sts, p1tbl, p1.

Work in pattern as est for a further 18 rows. Place all sts on waste yarn or stitch holder and break yarn. Place locking stitch marker in RS of work to help orient left back neck tab.

LEFT BACK NECK TAB

Carefully unpick provisional cast-on and place the 60 sts on larger circular needle. Join yarn, ready to work a WS row. You may now remove locking stitch marker.

Work 6 rows in garter stitch.

SET-UP ROW (WS): P1, p1tbl, [k1, p1tbl] to end.
ROW 1 (RS): [K1tbl, p1] to last 2 sts, k1tbl, k1.
ROW 2: P1, p1tbl, [k1, p1tbl] to end.

Work in pattern as est for a further 18 rows.

NEXT ROW (tab row) (RS): [K1tbl, p1] to last 2 sts, ssk, PM, turn work 90 degrees clockwise and with working needle, pick up and knit 49 sts in Neck Tabs, PM, turn work 90 degrees clockwise, replace held Right Back Neck Tab sts on left needle ready to work a RS row, k2tog, [p1, k1tbl] to end. *167 sts*
NEXT ROW (WS): [P1tbl, k1] to 1 st before marker, p1tbl, SM, p2, PM, [p1tbl, k1] to 3 sts before marker, p1tbl, PM, p2, SM, [p1tbl, k1] to last st, p1tbl.

BODY

ROW 1 (RS): Work row 1 of Cable Panel to marker, working bracketed repeat 4 times, SM, yo, knit to marker, backwards-yo, SM, work row 1 of Cable Panel to marker, working bracketed repeat 3 times, SM, yo, knit to marker, backwards-yo, SM, work row 1 of Cable Panel to end, working bracketed repeat 4 times. *4 sts inc*
ROW 2 (WS): [Work row 2 of Cable Panel as est to marker, SM, purl backwards-yo through the front loop, twisting it closed, purl to 1 st before marker, purl yo through the back loop, twisting it closed, SM] twice, work row 2 of Cable Panel to end.

Work in pattern as est for a further 22 rows, ending after row 24 of Cable Panel. *215 sts in the following configuration: 59 sts in Left Cable Panel, 26 sts in St st, 45 sts in Cable Panel at centre, 26 sts in St st, and 59 sts in Right Cable Panel.*
Work in pattern as est for a further 72 (96, 96, 96, 96, 96, 120, 120) rows, working rows 1-24 of Cable Panel a further 3 (4, 4, 4, 4, 4, 5, 5) times. *359 (407, 407, 407, 407, 407, 455, 455) sts in the following configuration: 59 sts in Left Cable Panel, 98 (122, 122, 122, 122, 122, 146, 146) sts in St st, 45 sts in Cable Panel at centre, 98 (122, 122, 122, 122, 122, 146, 146) sts in St st, and 59 sts in Right Cable Panel.*

Sizes 1 (-, 3, 4, 5, 6, -, 8) only:
Work in pattern as est for a further 16 (-, 4, 8, 16, 20, -, 4) rows, ending on row 16 (-, 4, 8, 16, 20, -, 4) of Cable Panel. *391 (-, 415, 423, 439, 447, -, 463) sts in the following configuration: 59 sts in Left Cable Panel, 114 (-, 126, 130, 138, 142, -, 150) sts in St st, 45 sts in Cable Panel at centre, 114 (-, 126, 130, 138, 142, -, 150) sts in St st, and 59 sts in Right Cable Panel.*

All sizes resume:
Break yarn and place the 59 sts before first marker (for Left Cable Panel) and the 59 sts after final marker (for Right Cable Panel) on separate waste yarn or stitch holders, removing those markers as you go. *273 (289, 297, 305, 321, 329, 337, 345) sts*

CHEVRON

ROW 1 (RS): K1, ssk, knit to marker, backwards-yo, SM, work row 17 (1, 5, 9, 17, 21, 1, 5) of Cable Panel as est to marker, SM, yo, knit to last 3 sts, k2tog, k1.
ROW 2 (WS): Purl to 1 st before marker, purl yo through the back loop, twisting it closed, SM, work row 18 (2, 6, 10, 18, 22, 2, 6) of Cable Panel as est to marker, SM, purl backwards-yo through the front loop, twisting it closed, purl to end.

Rep rows 1-2 a further 3 (11, 9, 7, 3, 1, 11, 9) time(s), ending after row 24 of Cable Panel.

Rep rows 1-2 a further 36 (36, 36, 48, 48, 60, 48, 48) times, working rows 1-24 of Cable Panel 3 (3, 3, 4, 4, 5, 4, 4) times.

Place the 45 Cable Panel sts and the 114 (122, 126, 130, 138, 142, 146, 150) sts after the Cable Panel when viewed from the RS on two separate stitch holders or pieces of waste yarn. *114 (122, 126, 130, 138, 142, 146, 150) sts ready to be worked for left bottom point*

LEFT BOTTOM POINT

ROW 1 (RS): K1, ssk, knit to last 3 sts, k2tog, k1. *2 sts dec*
ROW 2 (WS): Purl.
Rep rows 1-2 a further 54 (58, 60, 62, 66, 68, 70, 72) times. *4 sts*

Cast off all sts knitwise.

RIGHT BOTTOM POINT

Replace the 114 (122, 126, 130, 138, 142, 146, 150) held St st sts on larger circular needle, ready to work a RS row. Work as for Left Bottom Point.

BORDER

With RS facing, Left and Right Bottom Points at top and cable border at bottom, and using smaller needle, return the 59 held Left Cable Panel sts to left needle ready to work a RS row.

PICK-UP ROW (RS): [K1tbl, p1] to last st, k1tbl; pick up and knit 125 (143, 143, 159, 159, 171, 175, 175) sts along St st edge to tip of Left Bottom Point at a rate of approximately 2 sts every 3 rows; PM, pick up and knit 74 (80, 82, 84, 90, 92, 96, 98) sts along edge of Left Bottom Point to the held Cable Panel sts at a rate of approximately 2 sts every 3 rows; return the 45 Cable Panel sts to left needle and [k1tbl, p1] to last st, k1tbl, pick up and knit 74 (80, 82, 84, 90, 92, 96, 98) sts along edge to tip of Right Bottom Point at a rate of approximately 2 sts every 3 rows; PM, pick up and knit 125 (143, 143, 159, 159, 171, 175, 175) sts along St st edge to held Right Cable Panel sts, replace the 59 held Right Cable Panel sts on left needle and [k1tbl, p1] to last st, k1tbl. *561 (609, 613, 649, 661, 689, 705, 709) sts in the following configuration: 184 (202, 202, 218, 218, 230, 234, 234) sts in left edge, 193 (205, 209, 213, 225, 229, 237, 241) sts in bottom edge, and 184 (202, 202, 218, 218, 230, 234, 234) sts in right edge*

NEXT ROW (WS): [P1tbl, k1] to last st, p1tbl.
ROW 1 (RS): [K1tbl, p1] to marker, M1R, SM, k1tbl, M1L, [p1, k1tbl] to 2 sts before marker, p1, M1R, k1tbl, SM, M1L, [p1, k1tbl] to end. *4 sts inc*

ROW 2 (WS): [P1tbl, k1] to 1 st before marker, p1tbl, SM, (p1tbl) twice, [k1, p1tbl] to 3 sts before marker, k1, (p1tbl) twice, SM, p1tbl, [k1, p1tbl] to end.
ROW 3: [K1tbl, p1] to 1 st before marker, k1tbl, M1R, SM, k1tbl, M1L, [k1tbl, p1] to 2 sts before marker, k1tbl, M1R, k1tbl, SM, M1L, k1tbl, [p1, k1tbl] to end. *569 (617, 621, 657, 669, 697, 713, 717) sts*
ROW 4: [P1tbl, k1] to last st, p1tbl.
ROW 5: Rep row 1. *573 (621, 625, 661, 673, 701, 717, 721) sts in the following configuration: 187 (205, 205, 221, 221, 233, 237, 237) sts in left edge, 199 (211, 215, 219, 231, 235, 243, 247) sts in bottom edge, 187 (205, 205, 221, 221, 233, 237, 237) sts in right edge*

FINISHING

NEXT ROW (WS): Place locking stitch markers 59 sts in from each edge, at juncture of cable panel and rem border sts and work using a modified Jeny's Surprisingly Stretchy cast-off as follows: k1, *backwards-yo, k1, pass first 2 sts over third st; rep from * to locking stitch marker, remove marker, slip remaining cable panel st on right needle back to left needle, p2togtbl, (all 59 Right Cable Panel sts cast off), [k1, p1tbl] to 1 st before marker, k1, remove marker (128 (146, 146, 162, 162, 174, 178, 178) sts worked for Right Body), k1, *backwards-yo, k1, pass first 2 sts over third st; rep from * to marker, remove marker, slip remaining cable panel st on right needle back to left needle, p2togtbl (199 (211, 215, 219, 231, 235, 243, 247) bottom edge sts cast off), [k1, p1tbl] to 1 st before locking stitch marker, k1, remove marker (128 (146, 146, 162, 162, 174, 178, 178) sts worked for Left Body), k1, *backwards-yo, k1, pass first 2 sts over third st; rep from * to end, passing yarn through final cast-off st (all 59 Left Cable Panel sts cast off). *128 (146, 146, 162, 162, 174, 178, 178) sts on either side of body*

Place each set of sts on waste yarn and block piece to measurements.

CUFFS (BOTH ALIKE)

Return one set of 128 (146, 146, 162, 162, 174, 178, 178) sts to smaller needle and turn work so that WS is facing. Bring needle tips together and, using a three-needle cast-off, join together first 44 (51, 48, 53, 50, 53, 52, 49) sts on each needle tip. Turn work so that RS is facing and distribute remaining sts, including final cast-off st, onto needle suitable for working small circumferences. PM for beg of round. *41 (45, 51, 57, 63, 69, 75, 81) sts*

ROUND 1: With working yarn, k2tog first st and final cast-off st, p1, [k1tbl, p1] to end. *40 (44, 50, 56, 62, 68, 74, 80) sts*
ROUND 2: [K1tbl, p1] to end.
Work even in twisted rib as est for 4 more rounds.
Cast off all sts using the ssk cast-off method.
Weave in all ends and steam-block the three-needle cast-offs and cuffs.

VIONNET SCHEMATIC KEY

A. Back neck width/centre cable panel width: 18cm / 7"
B. Cable panel width: 24cm / 9½"
C. Body width: 90 (95, 98, 101, 106, 108, 111, 113)cm / 35½ (37½, 38½, 39½, 41½, 42½, 43½, 44½)"
D. Body length: 55 (67.5, 66.25, 72.5, 70, 76.25, 82.5, 81.25)cm / 21¾ (26½, 26, 28½, 27½, 30, 32½, 32)"
E. Shoulder: 49.5 (53, 55, 56.5, 60, 61.5, 63.5, 65)cm / 19½ (21, 21½, 22¼, 23½, 24¼, 25, 25¾)"
F. Three-needle cast-off length: 24.5 (28.5, 26.5, 29.5, 28, 29.5, 29, 27)cm / 9½ (11¼, 10½, 11½, 11, 11½, 11¼, 10¾)"
G. Armhole circumference: 23 (25, 28.5, 31.5, 35, 38.5, 41.5, 45)cm / 9 (9¾, 11¼, 12½, 13¾, 15, 16½, 17¾)"

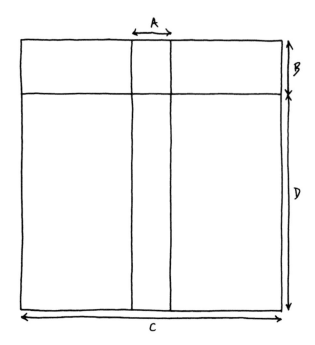

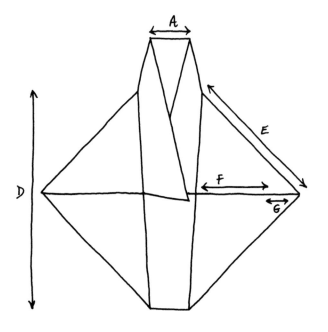

Cable Panel

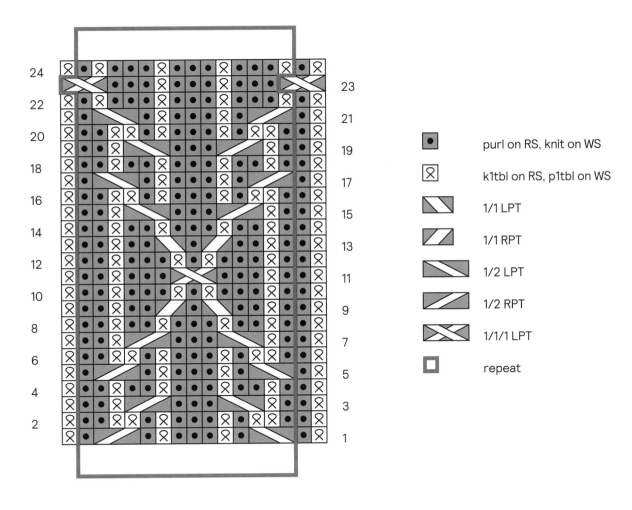

•	purl on RS, knit on WS
⊠	k1tbl on RS, p1tbl on WS
⟋	1/1 LPT
⟋	1/1 RPT
⟋	1/2 LPT
⟋	1/2 RPT
⟋⟍	1/1/1 LPT
▫	repeat

Overlap: Tomoko

When is a shawl not a shawl? Worked as for a traditional top-down shawl, the Tomoko cowl juxtaposes vivid brioche lace and stripes with a sleek overlapping construction and interesting angles.

Named after Tomoko Fuse, renowned as a master of modular origami.

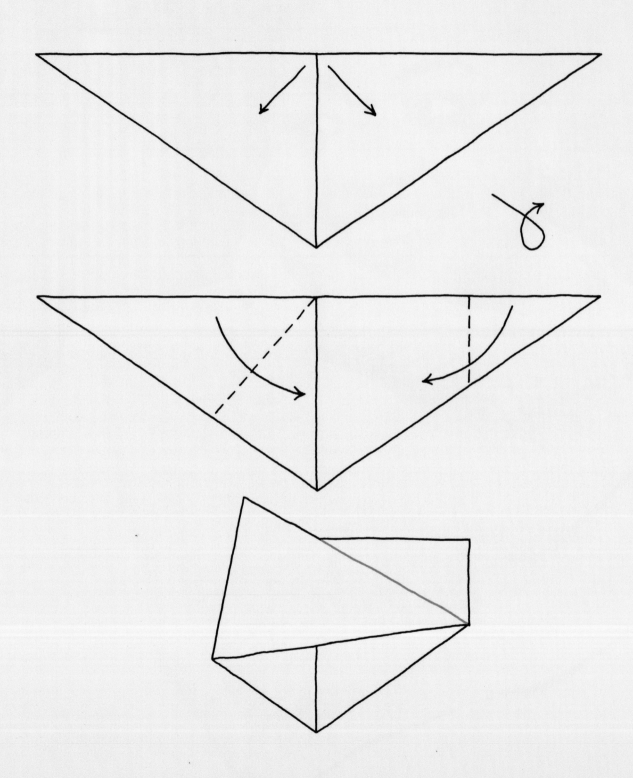

One size:

73cm / 28¾" circumference at narrowest point, 87cm / 34¼" circumference at widest point x 41cm / 16¼" deep

Yarn: North Light Fibers (pictured p43, p46, p47)

Water Street (DK weight; 60% super-fine Merino, 40% cashmere; 151m / 165yds per 57g skein)

Yarn A: Pussy Willow; 2 skeins
Yarn B: Pebble; 1 skein

OR

Yarn: The Farmer's Daughter Fibers (pictured p37)

Pishkun (DK weight; 100% Montana Rambouillet; 233m / 255yds per 100g skein)

Yarn A: Winter Wolf; 2 skeins
Yarn B: Chinook Winds; 1 skein

Gauge:

18 sts and 52 rows = 10cm / 4" over brioche pattern on 4mm needles after blocking.

Needles:

4mm / US 6 circular needle, 80cm / 32" length

Always use a needle size that will result in the correct gauge after blocking.

Notions:

2 locking stitch markers, tapestry needle

Notes:

Tomoko is started from a small number of stitches and increased every fourth row. After the piece is complete, it is partially cast off, and then overlapped and joined together during the remainder of the cast-off.

Stitch Glossary:

brk: Knit slipped st and yo together.
brp: Purl slipped st and yo together.
brkyobrk: Knit 1, keeping brk on left needle, yo around right needle, knit into brk once more and drop from left needle. *2 sts inc*
brkyobrkyobrk: *Knit 1, keeping brk on left needle, yo around right needle; rep from * once, knit into brk once more and drop from left needle. *4 sts inc*
dec-4: Slip 1 knit column as if to knit, slip next 2 columns together as if to knit, k1, pass the 2 columns over, return stitch to left needle, pass next column over, return stitch to right needle, pass the first column over. *4 sts dec*
sl1yo: Bring yarn to front between needles, slip next st purlwise, bring yarn over needle and slipped stitch. If working a knit afterwards, leave yarn in back ready to work a knit stitch; if working a purl afterwards, bring yarn to front between needles ready to work a purl.
Slide: In two-colour brioche, each row is worked twice, first with Yarn B then with Yarn A. At the end of each Yarn B row do not turn, but **slide** sts to other end of needle to work Yarn A row.

CHARTS – WRITTEN INSTRUCTIONS

SINGLE-COLOUR BRIOCHE

ROW 1 (RS): K1, sl1yo, (brkyobrk) into next st, sl1yo, [brk, sl1yo] to centre st, (brkyobrkyobrk) into centre st, remove locking st marker and place in new centre st, [sl1yo, brk] to last 4 sts, sl1yo, (brkyobrk) into next st, sl1yo, k1. *8 sts inc*

ROW 2 (WS): P1, brk, sl1yo, k1, [sl1yo, brk] to 2 sts before centre st [sl1yo, k1] twice, sl1yo, [brk, sl1yo] to last 4 sts, k1, sl1yo, brk, p1.
ROW 3: K1, sl1yo, [brk, sl1yo] to last st, k1.
ROW 4: P1, brk, [sl1yo, brk] to last st, p1.
ROW 5: K1, sl1yo, (brkyobrk) into next st, sl1yo, [brk, sl1yo] to last 3 sts, (brkyobrk) into next st, sl1yo, k1. *4 sts inc*
ROW 6: P1, brk, sl1yo, k1, [sl1yo, brk] to last 5 sts, sl1yo, k1, sl1yo, brk, p1.
ROW 7: Rep row 3.
ROW 8: Rep row 4.

TWO-COLOUR BRIOCHE
ROW 1 (RS, YARN B): K1, sl1yo, (brkyobrk) into next st, [sl1yo, brk] to 1 st before centre, sl1yo, (brkyobrkyobrk) into centre st, remove locking st marker and place in new centre st, sl1yo, [brk, sl1yo] to last 3 sts, (brkyobrk) into next st, sl1yo, k1. Slide. *8 sts inc*
ROW 2 (RS, YARN A): K1, brp, sl1yo, p1, sl1yo, [brp, sl1yo] to 1 st before centre st, p1, sl1yo, p1, [sl1yo, brp] to last 5 sts, sl1yo, p1, sl1yo, brp, k1. Turn.
ROW 3 (WS, YARN B): P1, [sl1yo, brp] to last 2 sts, sl1yo, p1. Slide.
ROW 4 (WS, YARN A): P1, [brk, sl1yo] to last 2 sts, brk, p1. Turn.
ROW 5 (RS, YARN B): K1, sl1yo, (brkyobrk) into next st, [sl1yo, brk] to last 4 sts, sl1yo, (brkyobrk) into next st, sl1yo, k1. Slide. *4 sts inc*
ROW 6 (RS, YARN A): K1, brp, sl1yo, p1, [sl1yo, brp] to last 5 sts, sl1yo, p1, sl1yo, brp, k1. Turn.
ROW 7 (WS, YARN B): Rep row 3.
ROW 8 (WS, YARN A): Rep row 4.
ROW 9 (RS, YARN B): K1, sl1yo, (brkyobrk) into next st, sl1yo, dec-4, [sl1yo, (brkyobrkyobrk) into next st, sl1yo, dec-4] to 3 sts before centre st, sl1yo, brk, sl1yo, (brkyobrkyobrk) into centre st, remove locking st marker and place in new centre st, sl1yo, brk, sl1yo, [dec-4, sl1yo, (brkyobrkyobrk) into next st, sl1yo] to last 9 sts, dec-4, sl1yo, (brkyobrk) into next st, sl1yo, k1. Slide. *8 sts inc*

ROW 10 (RS, YARN A): K1, brp, sl1yo, p1, sl1yo, brp, sl1yo, [brp, sl1yo, (p1, sl1yo) twice, brp, sl1yo] to 5 sts before centre st, [brp, sl1yo] twice, p1, sl1yo, p1, [sl1yo, brp] twice, [sl1yo, brp, (p1, sl1yo) twice, sl1yo, brp] to last 7 sts, sl1yo, brp, sl1yo, p1, sl1yo, brp, k1. Turn.

ROWS 11–16: Rep rows 3–8. *4 sts inc*

ROW 17 (RS, YARN B): K1, sl1yo, (brkyobrk) into next st, [sl1yo, brk] twice, [sl1yo, (brkyobrkyobrk) into next st, sl1yo, dec-4] to 5 sts before centre st, sl1yo, (brkyobrkyobrk) into next st, sl1yo, brk, sl1yo, (brkyobrkyobrk) into centre st, remove locking st marker and place in new centre st, sl1yo, brk, sl1yo, (brkyobrkyobrk) into next st, sl1yo, [dec-4, sl1yo, (brkyobrkyobrk) into next st, sl1yo] to last 7 sts, [brk, sl1yo] twice, (brkyobrk) into next st, sl1yo, k1. Slide. *8 sts inc*

ROW 18 (RS, YARN A): K1, brp, sl1yo, p1, [sl1yo, brp] twice, sl1yo, [brp, (sl1yo, p1) twice, sl1yo, brp, sl1yo] to 3 sts before centre st, brp, [sl1yo, p1] twice, sl1yo, brp, [sl1yo, brp, (sl1yo, p1) twice, sl1yo, brp] to last 9 sts, [sl1yo, brp] twice, sl1yo, p1, sl1yo, brp, k1. Turn.

ROWS 19–24: Rep rows 3–8. *4 sts inc*

ROW 25 (RS, YARN B): K1, sl1yo, (brkyobrk) into next st, sl1yo, dec-4, [sl1yo, (brkyobrkyobrk) into next st, sl1yo, dec-4] to 5 sts before centre st, sl1yo, (brkyobrkyobrk) into next st, sl1yo, brk, sl1yo, (brkyobrkyobrk) into centre st, remove locking st marker and place in new centre st, sl1yo, brk, sl1yo, (brkyobrkyobrk) into next st, sl1yo, [dec-4, sl1yo, (brkyobrkyobrk) into next st, sl1yo] to last 9 sts, dec-4, sl1yo, (brkyobrk) into next st, sl1yo, k1. Slide. *8 sts inc*

ROW 26 (RS, YARN A): K1, brp, sl1yo, p1, sl1yo, brp, sl1yo, [brp, (sl1yo, p1) twice, sl1yo, brp, sl1yo] to 3 sts before centre st, brp, [sl1yo, p1] twice, sl1yo, brp, [sl1yo, brp, (sl1yo, p1) twice, sl1yo, brp] to last 7 sts, sl1yo, brp, sl1yo, p1, sl1yo, brp, p1. Turn.

ROWS 27–32: Rep rows 3–8. *4 sts inc*

ROW 33 (RS, YARN B): K1, sl1yo, (brkyobrk) into next st, sl1yo, brk, sl1yo, dec-4, [sl1yo, (brkyobrkyobrk) into next st, sl1yo, dec-4] to 3 sts before centre st, sl1yo, (brkyobrkyobrk) into next st, sl1yo, (brkyobrkyobrk) into centre st, remove locking st marker and place in new centre st, sl1yo, (brkyobrkyobrk) into next st, [dec-4, sl1yo, (brkyobrkyobrk) into next st, sl1yo] to last 11 sts, dec-4, sl1yo, brk, sl1yo, (brkyobrk) into next st, sl1yo, k1. Slide. *8 sts inc*

ROW 34 (RS, YARN A): K1, brp, sl1yo, p1, [sl1yo, brp] twice, sl1yo, [brp, sl1yo, (p1, sl1yo) twice, brp, sl1yo] to 1 st before centre st, p1, sl1yo, p1, [sl1yo, brp, (sl1yo, p1) twice, sl1yo, brp], to last 9 sts, [sl1yo, brp] twice, sl1yo, p1, sl1yo, brp, k1. Turn.

ROWS 35–40: Rep rows 3–8. *4 sts inc*

PATTERN BEGINS

SET-UP

With Yarn A and using the long-tail method, cast on 5 sts.

SET-UP ROW (WS): Purl.
Work next 12 rows from Set-Up Chart or written instructions below.

ROW 1 (RS): [K1, (brkyobrk) into next st] twice, k1. *9 sts*

ROW 2 (WS): P1, [k1, sl1yo] 3 times, k1, p1.

ROW 3: K1, [sl1yo, brk] to last 2 sts, sl1yo, k1.

ROW 4: P1, [brk, sl1yo] to last 2 sts, brk, p1.

ROW 5: K1, sl1yo, (brkyobrk) into next st, sl1yo, (brkyobrkyobrk) into next st, sl1yo, (brkyobrk) into next st, sl1yo, k1. *17 sts*

ROW 6: P1, [brk, sl1yo, k1, sl1yo] twice, k1, sl1yo, brk, sl1yo, k1, sl1yo, brk, p1.

ROW 7: Rep row 3.

ROW 8: Rep row 4.

ROW 9: K1, sl1yo, (brkyobrk) into next st, [sl1yo, brk] to last 4 sts, sl1yo, (brkyobrk) into next st, sl1yo, k1. *21 sts*

ROW 10: P1, brk, sl1yo, k1, [sl1yo, brk] to last 5 sts, sl1yo, k1, sl1yo, brk, p1.

ROW 11: Rep row 3.

ROW 12: Rep row 4. Place locking stitch marker in centre stitch.

Work Single-Colour Brioche and Two-Colour Brioche by referring to the charts or the instructions in the Stitch Glossary.

SINGLE-COLOUR BRIOCHE
Work rows 1–8 of Single-Colour Brioche 3 times. *57 sts*
Place locking stitch marker in last row on right edge of fabric.

TWO-COLOUR BRIOCHE
Join Yarn B and work rows 1–24 of Two-Colour Brioche once. *93 sts*
Break Yarn B.

SINGLE-COLOUR BRIOCHE
Work rows 1–8 of Single-Colour Brioche 4 times. *141 sts*

TWO-COLOUR BRIOCHE
Join Yarn B and work rows 1–40 of Two-Colour Brioche once. *201 sts*
Break Yarn B.

SINGLE-COLOUR BRIOCHE
Work rows 1–8 of Single-Colour Brioche once. *213 sts*

TWO-COLOUR BRIOCHE
Join Yarn B and work rows 1–8 of Two-Colour Brioche once. *225 sts*
Break Yarn B.

SINGLE-COLOUR BRIOCHE
Work rows 1–8 of Single-Colour Brioche once. *237 sts*
Place locking stitch marker in centre stitch.

FINISHING

NEXT ROW (RS): With Yarn A, work a brioche modified Jeny's Surprisingly Stretchy cast-off over all sts to centre marker as follows: P1, *yo, brp, pass first two sts over third st, yo, p1, pass first two sts over third st; rep from * to 1 st before m, yo, brp, pass first two sts over third st, remove marker, yo, p1, pass first two sts over third st. Return final st to left needle; rep from * once more. *118 sts cast off, 119 sts rem*

Break Yarn A. Turn work so that WS is facing, and, using Yarn B and the cable method, cast on 3 sts. Turn work so that RS is facing.

I-CORD CAST-OFF, PART 1
ROW 1 (RS): With Yarn B, k2, ssk last Yarn B st with first Yarn A st, slip sts back to left needle. *1 Yarn A st dec*

ROW 2 (RS): With Yarn B, k3 Yarn B sts, slip sts back to left needle.

Rep these two rows 56 more times, then rep row 1 once more. *57 Yarn A sts dec, 60 Yarn A sts rem on needle*

I-CORD CAST-OFF, PART 2
Slide current stitches to end of left needle tip, ready to work a RS row. With right needle tip, starting at locking stitch marker in right edge of fabric, moving towards start of cast-off edge and using Yarn A, pick up and knit 60 sts at a rate of 1 st for every 2 rows. Break Yarn A. Slip newly picked-up sts to end of right needle tip, as if ready to join to work in the round.

ROW 1 (RS): With Yarn B, slip Yarn A st from right needle to left needle, k2tog with first Yarn B st, k1 Yarn B st, ssk last Yarn B sts with first Yarn A st, slip sts back to left needle. *1 st dec from either section of Yarn A sts*
ROW 2 (RS): With Yarn B, k3 Yarn B sts, slip sts back to left needle.
Rep these two rows 59 more times. *59 sts dec from either section of Yarn A sts, 3 Yarn B sts rem*

NEXT ROW (RS): Cast off rem 3 Yarn B sts knitwise.
Weave in all ends and block to measurements.

TOMOKO SCHEMATIC KEY

A. Full wingspan before joining: 118.5cm / 46¾"
B. Depth: 41cm / 16¼"
C. Circumference at narrowest point: 73cm / 28¾"
D. Circumference at widest point: 87cm / 34¼"

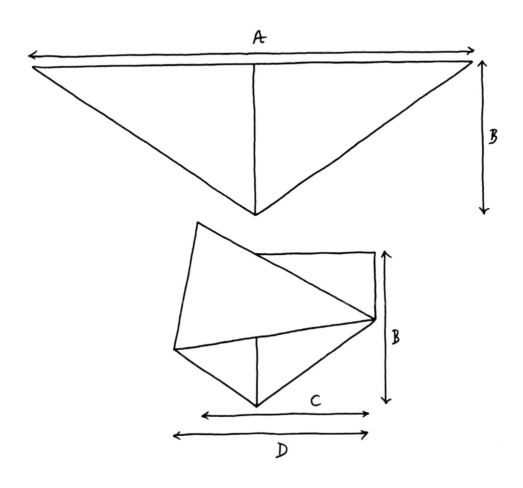

Single-Colour Brioche

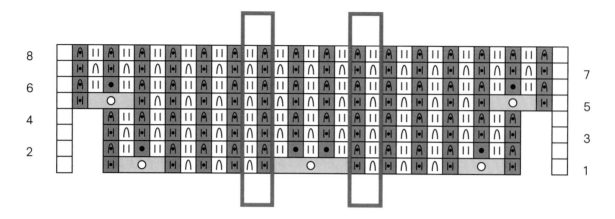

Set-Up Chart

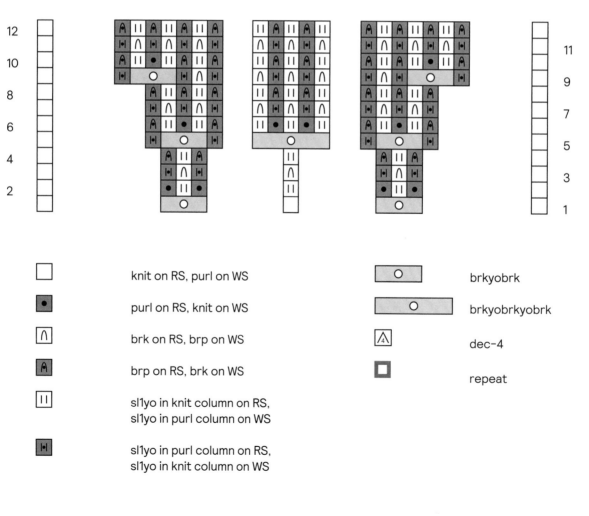

	knit on RS, purl on WS		brkyobrk
•	purl on RS, knit on WS		brkyobrkyobrk
∩	brk on RS, brp on WS	∕4	dec-4
A	brp on RS, brk on WS	☐	repeat
‖	sl1yo in knit column on RS, sl1yo in purl column on WS		
⦁⦁	sl1yo in purl column on RS, sl1yo in knit column on WS		

Two-Colour Brioche

This is one chart, split across two pages. When working RS rows, read from right (p45) to left (p44).
When working WS rows, read from left (p44) to right (p45).

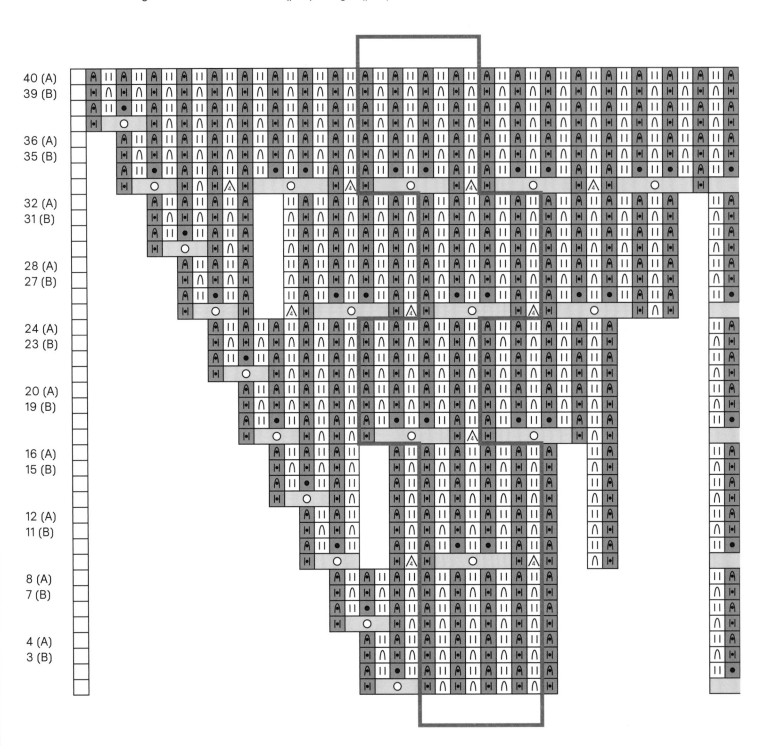

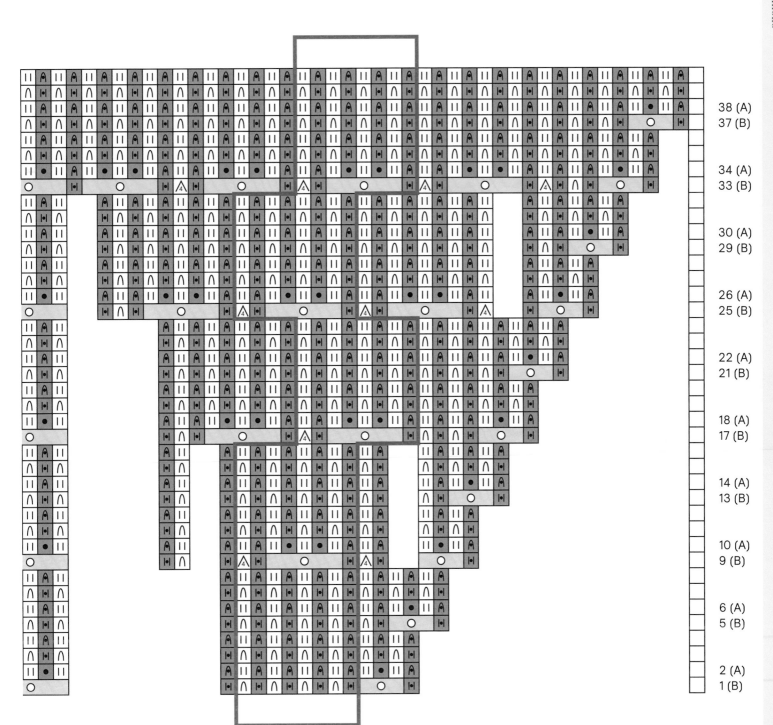

38 (A)
37 (B)

34 (A)
33 (B)

30 (A)
29 (B)

26 (A)
25 (B)

22 (A)
21 (B)

18 (A)
17 (B)

14 (A)
13 (B)

10 (A)
9 (B)

6 (A)
5 (B)

2 (A)
1 (B)

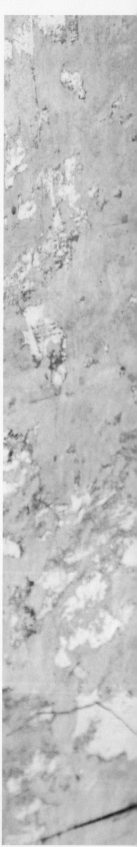

Rotate: Grès

The simple act of moving a seam from its traditional orientation can make a world of difference. In Grès, an unexpected angle joins deep pockets, saddle shoulders, bias construction, and lushly cabled sleeves to create an elegant step outside the norm.

Named after Madame Grès, a fashion designer whose hand-draped and pleated dresses were often created on the body to best follow the proportions and shape of the wearer.

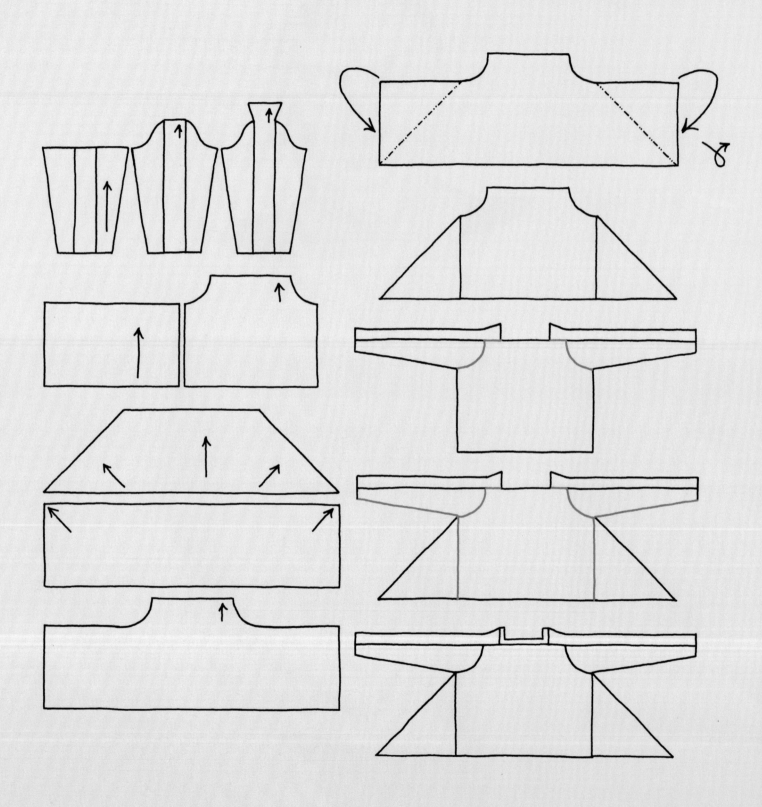

Sizes:

1 (2, 3, 4, 5, 6, 7, 8)

Finished bust circumference:

90 (102, 111, 123, 134, 146, 155, 167)cm / 35½ (40, 44, 48½, 53, 57½, 61, 65½)" – to be worn with 0-10cm / 0-4" positive ease

Model has 127cm / 50" bust, stands 175cm / 5'9" tall, and is wearing size 5.

Yarn: Moel View Yarn (pictured p49, p58, p60)

Infallible DK (DK weight, 55% Bluefaced Leicester, 45% silk; 212m / 232yds per 100g skein)

Shade: Oak Gall Grey; 7 (8, 9, 10, 11, 11, 12, 13) skeins

OR

Yarn: Neighborhood Fiber Co. (pictured p54, p59, p61)

Studio DK (DK weight, 100% superwash Merino; 251m / 275yds per 114g skein)

Shade: Charles Centre; 6 (7, 8, 8, 9, 10, 10, 11) skeins

Gauge:

21 sts & 29 rows = 10cm / 4" over stocking stitch on 3.5mm needles after blocking.

23 sts & 36 rows = 10cm / 4" over 1x1 rib pattern, stretched, on 3.5mm needles after blocking.

34-st x 32-row cable panel measures 9cm / 3½" wide x 10cm / 4" deep, on 4mm needles after blocking.

Needles:

4mm / US 6 circular needle, 80cm / 32" length, or straight needles

4mm / US 6 needle of preferred type for working small circumferences

3.5mm / US 4 circular needle, 40cm / 16" length

Always use a needle size that will result in the correct gauge after blocking.

Notions:

2 stitch markers, cable needle, 4 locking stitch markers, waste yarn, 2 stitch holders (optional), spare circular needle in same or smaller size as ribbing needle, tapestry needle

Notes:

Grès is knit in pieces and then seamed. Back and sleeves are shaped conventionally, with armhole and sleeve cap shaping, ending with a saddle. Front is worked with large wings on either side, worked by first increasing out to a large number of stitches on the bias, and then decreasing back down to a point.
Afterthought pockets are added when wings are at their widest point. The top edge of the wings are seamed to the side edges of the back when pieces are complete, which creates the drape in the body.
When Right and Left parts of the garment are referred to, they are the wearer's right and left.

Stitch Glossary:

2/3 LC: Sl 2 to cable needle, hold in front, k3, k2 from cable needle.
2/3 RC: Sl 3 to cable needle, hold in back, k2, k3 from cable needle.
3/3 LC: Sl 3 to cable needle, hold in front, k3, k3 from cable needle.

3/3 RC: Sl 3 to cable needle, hold in back, k3, k3 from cable needle.

SSK CAST-OFF: Ssk, *slip next st knitwise to right needle, insert left needle through front of both sts on right needle, k2togtbl; rep from * to end.

CHARTS – WRITTEN INSTRUCTIONS

CABLE PANEL

ROW 1 (RS): P2, 3/3 LC, p1, k1, p2, 2/3 LC, 2/3 RC, p2, k1, p1, 3/3 RC, p2.
ROW 2 (WS): K2, p6, k1, p1, k2, p10, k2, p1, k1, p6, k2.
ROW 3: P2, k6, p1, k1, p2, k10, p2, k1, p1, k6, p2.
ROW 4: Rep row 2.
ROWS 5-12: Rep rows 1-4 a further 2 times.
ROW 13: Rep row 1.
ROW 14: K2, p2, k1, p5, k2, p1, k1, p6, k1, p1, k2, p5, k1, p2, k2.
ROW 15: P2, k2, p1, k5, p2, k1, p1, k6, p1, k1, p2, k5, p1, k2, p2.
ROW 16: Rep row 14.
ROW 17: P2, k2, p1, 2/3 RC, p2, k1, p1, 3/3 LC, p1, k1, p2, 2/3 LC, p1, k2, p2.
ROWS 18-29: Rep rows 14-17 a further 3 times.
ROWS 30-32: Rep rows 2-4.

SADDLE PANEL

ALL SIZES:
ROW 1 (RS): K1, M1R, k4, p1, k1, p2, 2/3 LC, 2/3 RC, p2, k1, p1, k4, M1L, k1. *2 sts inc, 30 sts*
ROW 2 (WS): P6, k1, p1, k2, p10, k2, p1, k1, p6.
ROW 3: K1, M1R, k5, p1, k1, p2, k10, p2, k1, p1, k5, M1L, k1. *2 sts inc, 32 sts*
ROW 4: P7, k1, p1, k2, p10, k2, p1, k1, p7.
ROW 5: K1, 3/3 LC, p1, k1, p2, 2/3 LC, 2/3 RC, p2, k1, p1, 3/3 RC, k1.
ROW 6: Rep row 4.
ROW 7: K7, p1, k1, p2, k10, p2, k1, p1, k7.
ROW 8: Rep row 4.

ROW 9: K1, M1R, 3/3 LC, p1, k1, p2, 2/3 LC, 2/3 RC, p2, k1, p1, 3/3 RC, M1L, k1. *2 sts inc, 34 sts*
ROW 10: P8, k1, p1, k2, p10, k2, p1, k1, p8.
ROW 11: K8, p1, k1, p2, k10, p2, k1, p1, k8.
ROW 12: Rep row 10.
ROW 13: K2, 3/3 LC, p1, k1, p1, M1P, p1, 2/3 LC, 2/3 RC, p1, M1P, p1, k1, p1, 3/3 RC, k2. *2 sts inc, 36 sts*
ROW 14: P4, k1, p5, k3, p1, k1, p6, k1, p1, k3, p5, k1, p4.
ROW 15: K4, p1, k5, p3, k1, p1, k6, p1, k1, p3, k5, p1, k4.
ROW 16: Rep row 14.

SIZES – (–, 3, 4, 5, 6, 7, 8) ONLY:
ROW 17: K3, M1R, k1, p1, 2/3 RC, p3, k1, p1, 3/3 LC, p1, k1, p3, 2/3 LC, p1, k1, M1L, k3. *2 sts inc, 38 sts*
ROW 18: P5, k1, p5, k3, p1, k1, p6, k1, p1, k3, p5, k1, p5.

SIZES – (–, –, –, 5, 6, 7, 8) ONLY:
ROW 19: K5, p1, k5, p3, k1, M1P, p1, k6, p1, M1P, k1, p3, k5, p1, k5. *40 sts*
ROW 20: P5, k1, p5, k3, p1, k2, p6, k2, p1, k3, p5, k1, p5.

SIZES – (–, –, –, –, –, 7, 8) ONLY:
ROW 21: K5, p1, 2/3 RC, p3, M1R, k1, p2, 3/3 LC, p2, k1, M1L, p3, 2/3 LC, p1, k5. *42 sts*
ROW 22: P5, k1, p5, k3, p2, k2, p6, k2, p2, k3, p5, k1, p5.

PATTERN BEGINS

SLEEVES (BOTH ALIKE)

Using smaller needle and the long-tail tubular method, cast on 52 sts.
Do not join.

NEXT ROW (RS): [K1, sl1wyif] to end.
NEXT ROW (WS): [K1, sl1wyif] to end.

RIBBING
ROW 1 (RS): [K1, p1] 13 times, [p1, k1] 13 times.
ROW 2 (WS): [P1, k1] 13 times, [k1, p1] 13 times.

Work in pattern as est until work measures 5cm / 2" from cast-on edge, ending after a WS row.

SIZES 1, 2, 3, 4 ONLY:
NEXT ROW (RS): [K1, p1] 6 times, k1, PM, pfb, kfb, [p1, k1] 3 times, pfb, k1, p1, kfb, p2, kfb, p1, k1, pfb, [k1, p1] 3 times, kfb, pfb, PM, k1, [p1, k1] 6 times. *60 sts*
NEXT ROW (WS): [P1, k1] to 1 st before marker, p1, SM, k2, p2, k1, p5, k2, p1, k1, p6, k1, p1, k2, p5, k1, p2, k2, SM, p1, [k1, p1] to end.

SIZES 5, 6, 7, 8 ONLY:
NEXT ROW (RS): [K1, p1] 6 times, k1, PM, pfb, k2, kfb, [p1, k1] twice, pfb, kfb, [p1, k1, p1] twice, kfb, pfb, [k1, p1] twice, kfb, k2, pfb, PM, k1, [p1, k1] 6 times. *60 sts*
NEXT ROW (WS): [P1, k1] to 1 st before marker, p1, SM, k2, p4, [k1, p1] twice, k2, p2, [k1, p1, k1] twice, p2, k2, [p1, k1] twice, p4, k2, SM, p1, [k1, p1] to end.

ALL SIZES AGAIN:
Switch to larger needle.

ROW 1 (RS): Knit to marker, SM, work row 25 (21, 19, 17, 11, 7, 3, 31) of Cable Panel to marker, SM, knit to end.
ROW 2 (WS): Purl to marker, SM, work row 26 (22, 20, 18, 12, 8, 4, 32) of Cable Panel to marker, SM, purl to end.

Work even in St st and Cable Panel (starting back at row 1 after completing row 32 as needed) as est for a further 10 (6, 4, 2, 2, 0, 0, 0) rows.

Inc Row (RS): K1, M1L, work in pattern as est to last st, M1R, k1. *2 sts inc*

Rep Inc Row every 14 (10, 8, 6, 6, 4, 4, 4) th row a further 7 (7, 10, 7, 19, 4, 13, 22) times, then every 16 (12, 10, 8, 8, 6, 6, 6) th row 1 (4, 4, 10, 1, 18, 12, 6) time(s). *78 (84, 90, 96, 102, 106, 112, 118) sts*

Work even in St st and Cable Panel as est for 1 more row. Final row of Cable Panel worked should be row 24 (20, 18, 14, 10, 6, 2, 30).

SLEEVE CAP
Continuing in St st and Cable Panel as est, at beginning of next 2 rows, cast off 3 (3, 4, 4, 5, 5, 6, 6) sts knitwise. *72 (78, 82, 88, 92, 96, 100, 106) sts*

ROW 1 (RS): K1, ssk, work in pattern as est to last 3 sts, k2tog, k1. *2 sts dec*
ROW 2 (WS): P1, p2tog, purl to last 3 sts, ssp, p1. *2 sts dec*

Note: the final decreases of this section will eat into the edges of the cable panel. Omit stitches from the edge of the pattern as necessary.

Rep rows 1-2 a further 2 (3, 4, 5, 5, 5, 5, 6) times, then rep row 1 every RS row 16 (17, 17, 18, 20, 22, 24, 25) times, ending after a WS row. *28 sts*

Final row of Cable Panel worked should be row 32. Remove markers on final row.

SADDLE
ROW 1 (RS): Work row 1 of Saddle Panel.
ROW 2 (WS): Work row 2 of Saddle Panel.

Continue in pattern as est until row 16 (16, 18, 18, 20, 20, 22, 22) of Saddle Panel is completed. *36 (36, 38, 38, 40, 40, 42, 42) sts*

Cast off all sts knitwise.

BACK

Using smaller needle and the long-tail tubular method, cast on 97 (109, 119, 131, 143, 155, 165, 177) sts. Do not join.

NEXT ROW (RS): [K1, sl1wyif] to last st, k1.
NEXT ROW (WS): [Sl1wyif, k1] to last st, sl1wyif.

RIBBING
ROW 1 (RS): [K1, p1] to last st, k1.
ROW 2 (WS): [P1, k1] to last st, p1.
Rep rows 1-2 until work measures
3.75cm / 1½" from cast-on edge,
ending after a WS row.

BODY
Switch to larger needle.

Beg with a RS knit row, work even in
St st until work measures 35.5 (35.5,
36.75, 36.75, 36.75, 38, 40.75, 43.25)cm /
14 (14, 14½, 14½, 14½, 15, 16, 17)" from
cast-on edge, ending after a WS row.

ARMHOLE SHAPING
Continuing in St st, at beginning of next
2 rows, cast off 3 (3, 4, 4, 5, 5, 6, 6) sts
knitwise. *91 (103, 111, 123, 133, 145, 153,
165) sts*

ROW 1 (RS): K1, ssk, knit to last 3 sts,
k2tog, k1. *2 sts dec*
ROW 2 (WS): P1, p2tog, purl to last
3 sts, ssp, p1. *2 sts dec*

Rep rows 1-2 a further 0 (1, 2, 4, 6, 8,
10, 13) time(s), then rep row 1 every
RS row 6 (8, 9, 9, 9, 9, 9, 9) times,
then rep row 1 every 4th row 3 (4, 4,
4, 4, 4, 4, 4) times. *69 (71, 73, 77, 79,
83, 83, 83) sts*

Work even in St st as est until work
measures 12.5 (14.5, 15, 16.5, 18, 19.5,
20.5, 22)cm / 5 (5¾, 6, 6½, 7, 7½, 8¼,
8¾)" from first armhole shaping row,
ending after a WS row.

Cast off all sts using the ssk cast-off
method.

Place a locking stitch marker 13
(13, 14, 14, 15, 16, 16, 16) sts in from
each edge.

FRONT

Using smaller needle and the long-tail
tubular method, cast on 103 (115, 125,
137, 149, 161, 171, 183) sts. Do not join.

NEXT ROW (RS): [K1, sl1wyif] to last st, k1.

NEXT ROW (WS): [Sl1wyif, k1] to last st,
sl1wyif.

RIBBING
ROW 1 (RS): K1, M1R, p1, M1L, k1, PM,
[p1, k1] to last 4 sts, p1, PM, k1, M1R, p1,
M1L, k1. *107 (119, 129, 141, 153, 165, 175,
187) sts*
ROW 2 (WS): P2, k1, p2, SM, [k1, p1] to
1 st before marker, k1, SM, p2, k1, p2.
ROW 3: K1, M1R, [k1, p1] to 2 sts before
marker, k1, M1L, k1, SM, [p1, k1] to 1 st
before marker, p1, SM, k1, M1R, [k1, p1]
to 2 sts before end, k1, M1L, k1. *4 sts inc*
ROW 4: [P1, k1] to 1 st before marker,
p1, SM, [k1, p1] to 1 st before marker, k1,
SM, [k1, p1] to 1 st before end, p1.
ROW 5: K1, M1R, [p1, k1] to 2 sts before
marker, p1, M1L, k1, SM, [p1, k1] to 1 st
before marker, p1, SM, k1, M1R, [p1, k1]
to 2 sts before end, p1, M1L, k1. *4 sts inc*
ROW 6: P2, [k1, p1] to 3 sts before
marker, k1, p2, SM, [k1, p1] to 1 st
before marker, k1, SM, p2, [k1, p1] to
3 sts before end, k1, p2.

Rep rows 3-6 once more, then rep
rows 3-4 once more. *127 (139, 149, 161,
173, 185, 195, 207) sts in the following
configuration: 15 sts in each Side
Panel, 97 (109, 119, 131, 143, 155, 165, 177)
sts in Centre Panel.*

BODY
Switch to larger needles.

ROW 1 (RS): [K1, p1] 4 times, M1R, knit to
1 st before marker, M1L, k1, SM, knit to
marker, SM, M1R, knit to last 8 sts, M1L,
[p1, k1] 4 times. *4 sts inc*

ROW 2 (WS): [P1, k1] 4 times, purl to last
8 sts, [k1, p1] 4 times.

Rep rows 1-2 a further 46 (46, 48, 48,
48, 50, 53, 57) times. *315 (327, 345, 357,
369, 389, 411, 439) sts in the following
configuration: 109 (109, 113, 113, 113, 117,
123, 131) sts in either Side Panel, 97
(109, 119, 131, 143, 155, 165, 177) sts in
Centre Panel.*

LEFT SIDE PANEL POCKET PLACEMENT
ROW 1 (RS): [K1, p1] 4 times, k22 (22,
24, 24, 24, 25, 28, 31), then, with waste
yarn, k34, slip these sts on new yarn
back to left needle, ready to work
again; knit these sts with working yarn,
k37 (37, 39, 39, 39, 42, 45, 50) to 8 sts
before marker, [p1, k1] 4 times. Remove
marker; place all Centre Panel sts on a
stitch holder or length of waste yarn
and place Right Side Panel on another
stitch holder or length of waste yarn.
*109 (109, 113, 113, 113, 117, 123, 131) sts
on needle*
ROW 2 (WS): [P1, k1] 4 times, purl to last
8 sts, [k1, p1] 4 times.

LEFT SIDE PANEL
ROW 1: [K1, p1] 4 times, ssk, knit to last
10 sts, k2tog, [p1, k1] 4 times. *2 sts dec*
ROW 2: [P1, k1] 4 times, purl to last 8
sts, [k1, p1] 4 times.

Rep rows 1-2 a further 44 (44, 46, 46,
46, 48, 51, 55) times. *19 sts*

ROW 1 (RS): [K1, p1] 4 times, s2kpo,
[p1, k1] 4 times. *2 sts dec*
ROW 2 (WS): [P1, k1] to last st, p1.
ROW 3: [K1, p1] 3 times, k1, s2kpo, k1,
[p1, k1] to end. *2 sts dec*
ROW 4: [P1, k1] 3 times, p3, [k1, p1]
3 times.
ROW 5: [K1, p1] 3 times, s2kpo, [p1, k1]
to end. *2 sts dec*
ROW 6: [P1, k1] to last st, p1.
ROWS 7-10: Rep rows 3-6, working
bracketed repeats twice. *9 sts*

ROWS 11–14: Rep rows 3–6, working bracketed repeats once. *5 sts*
ROW 15: K1, s2kpo, k1. *3 sts*
ROW 16: Purl.

Cast off all sts knitwise.

RIGHT SIDE PANEL POCKET PLACEMENT
Return the 109 (109, 113, 113, 113, 117, 123, 131) held Right Side Panel sts to larger needle, ready to work a RS row.
ROW 1 (RS): [K1, p1] 4 times, k37 (37, 39, 39, 39, 42, 45, 50), then, with waste yarn, k34, slip these sts on new yarn back to left needle, ready to work again; knit these sts with working yarn, k22 (22, 24, 24, 24, 25, 28, 31), [p1, k1] 4 times.
ROW 2 (WS): [P1, k1] 4 times, purl to last 8 sts, [k1, p1] 4 times.

Work as for Left Side Panel.

FRONT YOKE
Return the 97 (109, 119, 131, 143, 155, 165, 177) held Centre Panel sts to larger needle, ready to work a RS row.
Work as for Back, from start of Armhole Shaping.

POCKETS (BOTH ALIKE)

With RS facing, and using larger needle in preferred method for small-circumference knitting, start at the right edge of pocket stitches, and carefully pick up (but do not knit) 34 sts in the row below the waste yarn (if they get twisted you can remount them before knitting). Then do the same with 34 sts in the row above the waste yarn. Remove the waste yarn, join to work in the round, and PM for beg of round. *68 sts*

SET-UP ROUND: P34, pick up and purl stitch in gap between rows, k34, pick up and knit stitch in gap between rows. *70 sts*

ROUND 1: [K34, sl1wyif] twice.
ROUND 2: Knit to end.

Work in pattern as est until work measures 12.75cm / 5" from pick-up, ending after a round 2.

Flip pocket so that WS is facing you and RS are together, and, using spare needle, close using three-needle cast-off.

FINISHING

Block all pieces to measurements.

Beginning where indicated by locking stitch marker, seam saddle and sleeve cap into place, and then seam sleeve and side seam. On the sides, start at the join between the side and centre panels, and end with the decrease section.

NECKBAND
With smaller needle and starting at the join between right back saddle and right back, pick up and knit 45 (47, 47, 51, 51, 53, 53, 53) sts in back neck cast-off, 27 (27, 29, 29, 30, 30, 32, 32) sts in saddle cast-off at a rate of approx 3 sts every 4 cast-off sts, 45 (47, 47, 51, 51, 53, 53, 53) sts in front neck cast-off, and 27 (27, 29, 29, 30, 30, 32, 32) sts in saddle cast-off at a rate of approx 3 sts every 4 cast-off sts. Join to work in the round, slip 1 st purlwise from right needle to left needle, and PM for beg of round. *144 (148, 152, 160, 162, 166, 170, 170) sts*

NEXT ROUND: K2tog, [p1, k1] to 2 sts before end of back neck sts, p1, k2tog, [p1, k1] to 2 (2, 2, 2, 1, 1, 1, 1) sts before end of left saddle sts, p2tog 1 (1, 1, 1, 0, 0, 0, 0) time(s), p1 0 (0, 0, 0, 1, 1, 1, 1) time(s), k2tog, [p1, k1] to 3 sts before end of front neck sts, p1, k2tog, p2tog 1 (1, 1, 1, 0, 0, 0, 0) time(s), p1 0 (0, 0, 0, 1, 1, 1, 1) time(s), [k1, p1] to end of round. *138 (142, 146, 154, 158, 162, 166, 166) sts*

RIBBING
ROUND 1: [K1, p1] to end.

Work in pattern as est until rib measures 3.75cm / 1½".

TUBULAR CAST-OFF
Hold spare needle tip parallel with and behind right-hand needle. Slip alternating sts to each needle: knit sts to front needle, purl sts to back needle. When all sts are separated, continue to hold needles parallel and graft together using Kitchener stitch.

GRÈS SCHEMATIC KEY

A. Cuff width: 22.5cm / 9"

B. Upper arm width: 30 (33, 35.5, 38.5, 41.5, 43.5, 46, 49)cm / 11¾ (13, 14, 15¼, 16¼, 17, 18¼, 19¼)"

C. Sleeve length: 49.75cm / 19½"

D. Sleeve cap/armhole depth: 12.5 (14.5, 15, 16.5, 18, 19.5, 20.5, 22)cm / 5 (5¾, 6, 6½, 7, 7½, 8¼, 8¾)"

E. Saddle length: 7.5 (7.5, 8.5, 8.5, 9.5, 9.5, 10.5, 10.5)cm / 3 (3, 3¼, 3¼, 3¾, 3¾, 4, 4)"

F. Saddle width: 9.5 (9.5, 10, 10, 10.5, 10.5, 11, 11)cm / 3¾ (3¾, 4, 4, 4¼, 4¼, 4½, 4½)"

G. Back width: 45 (51, 55.5, 61.5, 67, 73, 77.5, 83.5)cm / 17¾, 20, 22, 24¼, 26½, 28¾, 30½, 32¾)"

H. Body length to underarm: 35.5 (35.5, 36.75, 36.75, 36.75, 38, 40.75, 43.25)cm / 17 (19¼, 20¾, 23, 25, 27¼, 28¾, 31)"

I. Side panel hypotenuse: 52 (52, 54, 54, 54, 55.5, 58.5, 62.5)cm / 20½ (20½, 21¼, 21¼, 21¼, 22, 23, 24½)"

J. Side panel width: 36.5 (36.5, 38, 38, 38, 39.5, 41.5, 44)cm / 14½ (14½, 15, 15, 15, 15½, 16¼, 17¼)"

K. Height below pocket: 10.5 (10.5, 11.5, 11.5, 11.5, 12, 13.5, 15)cm / 4¼ (4¼, 4½, 4½, 4½, 43/4, 5¼, 6)"

L. Pocket width: 16cm / 6¼" (depth: 12.75cm / 5")

M. Height above pocket: 17.5 (17.5, 18.5, 18.5, 18.5, 20, 21.5, 24)cm / 7 (7, 7¼, 7¼, 7¼, 73/4, 8½, 9¼)"

N. Neck band width: 3.75cm / 1½"

O. Neck circumference: 60 (61.5, 63.5, 67, 68.5, 70.5, 72, 72)cm / 23½ (24¼, 25, 26¼, 27, 27¾, 28½, 28½)"

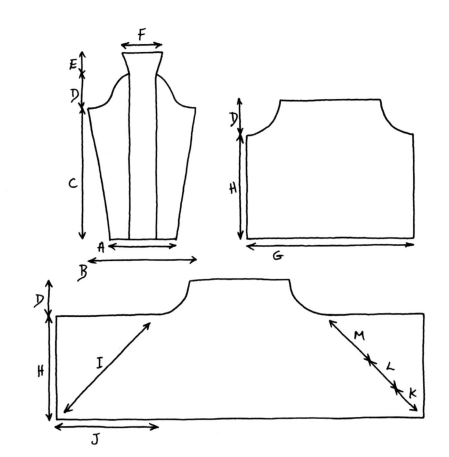

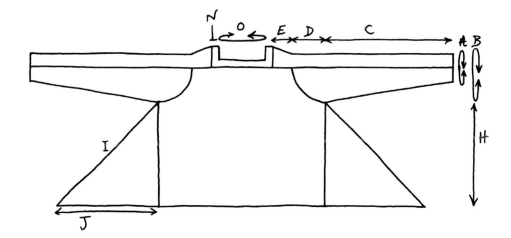

Cable Panel

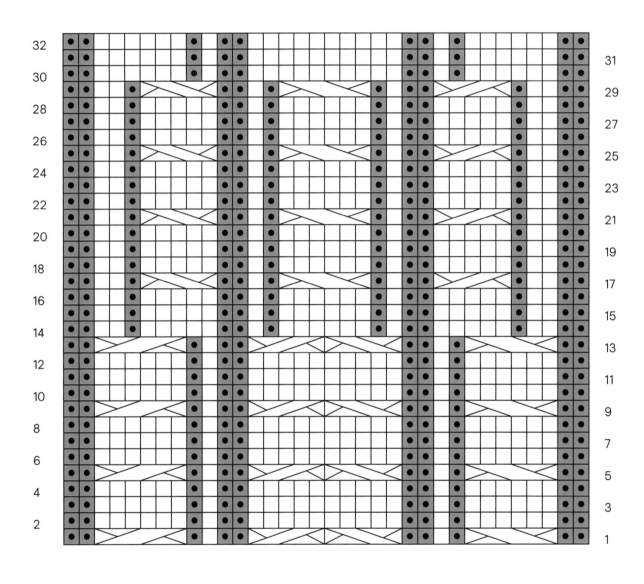

Saddle Panel

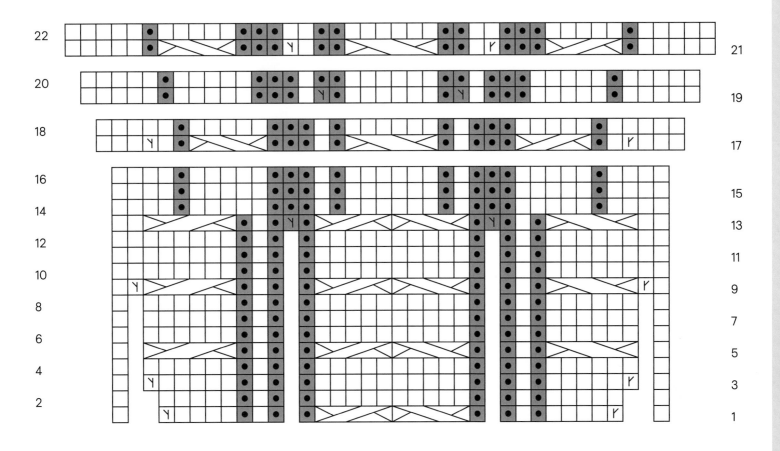

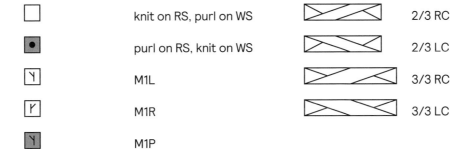

☐	knit on RS, purl on WS
⬤	purl on RS, knit on WS
Ɣ	M1L
⅄	M1R
▨	M1P

2/3 RC	
2/3 LC	
3/3 RC	
3/3 LC	

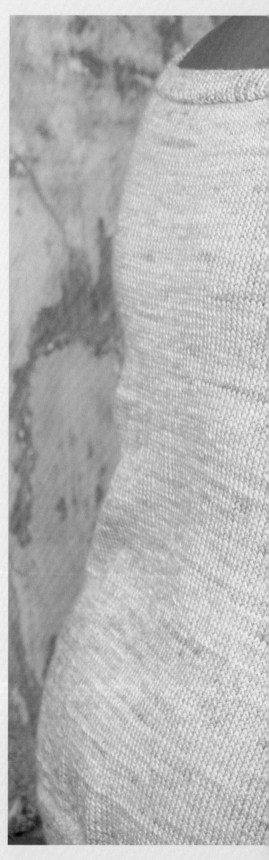

Twist: Mihara

A true and utter 'what if', Mihara
explores what might happen if a long
strip of fabric were twisted on itself and
around a body. Marrying cabled lace
and elongated garter stitch, it has drape
and fascinating construction for days.

*Named after Linda Tomoko Mihara, a contemporary origami
artist known for her work folding multiple interlocking cranes
out of a single sheet of paper.*

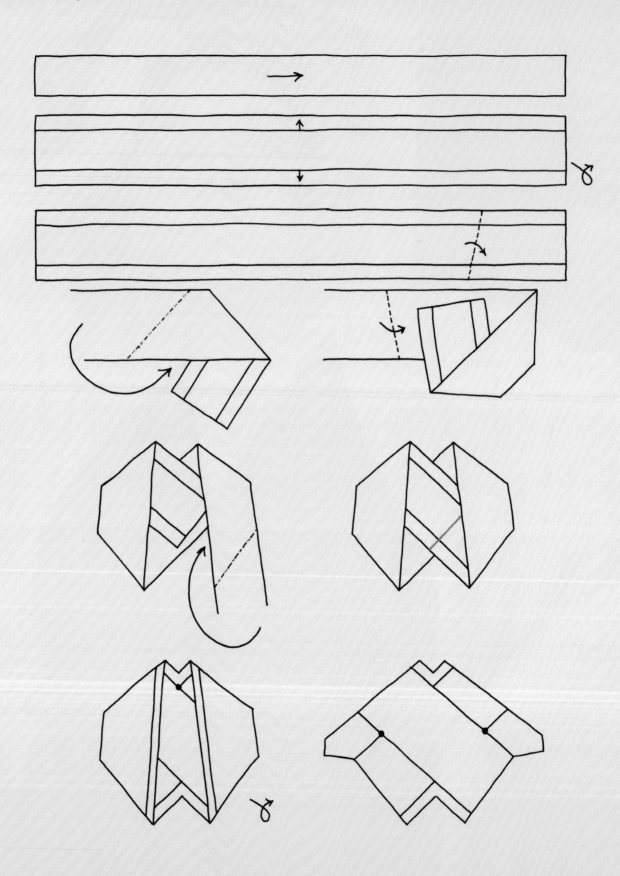

Sizes:

1 (2, 3, 4, 5, 6, 7, 8)

Finished back width:

47.5 (50.5, 52, 55, 57, 61, 63.5, 66.5)cm / 18¾ (19¾, 20½, 21¾, 22½, 24, 25, 26¼)" back width, to fit 76-86 (86.5-96, 96.5 -106, 106.5-116, 116.5-126, 127-139, 137-146, 146.5-157)cm / 30-33¾ (34-37¾, 38-41¾, 42-45¾, 46-49¾, 50-54¾, 54-57¾, 58-61¾)" bust circumference

Model has 127cm / 50" bust, stands 175cm / 5'9" tall, and is wearing size 5.

Yarn: CoopKnits (pictured p69, p71)

Socks Yeah! (light fingering/4-ply weight; 75% superwash Merino, 25% nylon; 212m / 231yds per 50g skein)

Shade: Danburite (105); 7 (7, 7, 8, 8, 8, 9, 9) skeins

OR

Yarn: Three Fates (pictured p63, p70)

Eponymous (fingering/4-ply weight; 100% superwash Merino; 366m / 400yds per 100g skein)

Shade: Excalibur; 4 (4, 5, 5, 5, 5, 5) skeins

Gauge:

21 sts & 42 rows/rounds = 10cm / 4" over elongated garter stitch on 3.75mm needles after blocking.

32 sts & 32 rows/rounds = 10cm / 4" over lace panel on 3.75mm needles after blocking.

Needles:

3.75mm / US 5 circular needle, 80cm / 32" length

3.75mm / US 5 circular needle, 40cm / 16" length

3.75mm / US 5 needle of preferred type for working small circumferences

Always use a needle size that will result in the correct gauge after blocking.

Notions:

4 stitch markers, cable needle, stitch holders or scrap yarn, tapestry needle, locking stitch markers or safety pins

Notes:

Mihara is started as one long strip, first worked from end to end, and then with stitches picked up along each long side. Once the edges are complete, stitches are put on hold for the body opening and the sleeve openings, the remainder of the stitches are cast off, and a full twist is introduced into the fabric. The strip is then seamed, keeping the twist in place. Once this is complete, held stitches are replaced on the needle and the border around the body opening is worked in the round. Following this, the held sleeve stitches are replaced on the needle and worked in the round.

Stitch Glossary:

1/2 LC: Sl 1 to cable needle, hold in front, k2, k1 from cable needle.
1/2 RC: Sl 2 to cable needle, hold in back, k1, k2 from cable needle.
1/3 LC: Sl 1 to cable needle, hold in front, k3, k1 from cable needle.
1/3 RC: Sl 3 to cable needle, hold in back, k1, k3 from cable needle.

ELONGATED GARTER STITCH

ROW 1 (RS): Knit.
ROW 2 (WS): Knit.
ROWS 3-4: Rep rows 1-2.
ROW 5: [K1, yo] to last st, k1.
ROW 6: [K1, drop yo] to last st, k1. This will elongate the stitches in the row below.
ROWS 7-8: Rep rows 1-2.

SSK CAST-OFF: Ssk, *slip next st knitwise to right needle, insert left needle through front of both sts on right needle, k2togtbl; rep from * to end.

CHARTS – WRITTEN INSTRUCTIONS

LACE PANEL (FLAT)

Note: Each double yo is treated as 2 sts on the next round/row.

ROW 1 (RS): K2, p1, 1/3 RC, 1/3 LC, [p1, k8, p1, 1/3 RC, 1/3 LC] twice, p1, k2.
ROW 2: P2, k1, [p8, k1] 5 times, p2.
ROW 3: K2, p1, k1, 1/2 RC, 1/2 LC, k1, [p1, k8, p1, k1, 1/2 RC, 1/2 LC, k1] twice, p1, k2.
ROW 4: Rep row 2.
ROW 5: K2, p1, k2, k2tog, (yo) twice, ssk, k2, [p1, k8, p1, k2, k2tog, (yo) twice, ssk, k2] twice, p1, k2.
ROW 6: P2, k1, [p3, (k1, p1) into double yo, p3, k1, p8, k1] twice, p3, (k1, p1) into double yo, p3, k1, p2.
ROW 7: K2, p1, k8, [p1, 1/3 RC, 1/3 LC, p1, k8] twice, p1, k2.
ROW 8: Rep row 2.
ROW 9: K2, p1, k8, [p1, k1, 1/2 RC, 1/2 LC, k1, p1, k8] twice, p1, k2.
ROW 10: Rep row 2.
ROW 11: K2, p1, k8, [p1, k2, k2tog, (yo) twice, ssk, k2, p1, k8] twice, p1, k2.
ROW 12: P2, k1, [p8, k1, p3, (k1, p1) into double yo, p3, k1] twice, p8, k1, p2.

LACE PANEL (IN THE ROUND)

ROUND 1: K8, p1, 1/3 RC, 1/3 LC, p1.
ROUND 2: [K8, p1] twice.
ROUND 3: K8, p1, k1, 1/2 RC, 1/2 LC, k1, p1.
ROUND 4: Rep round 2.
ROUND 5: K8, p1, k2, k2tog, (yo) twice, ssk, k2, p1.
ROUND 6: K8, p1, k3, (k1, p1) into double yo, k3, p1.
ROUND 7: 1/3 RC, 1/3 LC, p1, k8, p1.
ROUND 8: Rep round 2.
ROUND 9: K1, 1/2 RC, 1/2 LC, k1, p1, k8, p1.
ROUND 10: Rep round 2.
ROUND 11: K2, k2tog, (yo) twice, ssk, k2, p1, k8, p1.
ROUND 12: K3, (k1, p1) into double yo, k3, p1, k8, p1.

PATTERN BEGINS

CENTRE PANEL

Using the long-tail method, cast on 50 sts.
SET-UP ROW (WS): P2, [k1, p8] 5 times, k1, p2.

LACE PANEL

Working either from charted or written instructions, work rows 1–12 of Lace Panel 50 (53, 55, 58, 60, 64, 67, 70) times. (After blocking, this should measure approx 187.5 (198.75, 206.25, 217.5, 225, 240, 251.25, 262.5)cm / 73¾ (78¼, 81¼, 85¾, 88½, 94½, 99, 103¼)".)

Cast off all sts using modified Jeny's Surprisingly Stretchy cast-off as follows: K1, *backwards-yo, k1, slip first 2 sts over third; rep from * to end.

TOP EDGE

With RS facing, along right edge of Lace Panel, working from cast-on edge towards cast-off edge, pick up and knit 396 (432, 468, 504, 540, 576, 612, 648) sts. Do not join.
NEXT ROW (WS): Knit.

ROW 1 (RS): Knit.
ROW 2 (WS): Knit.
ROWS 3–4: Rep rows 1–2.
ROW 5: [K1, yo] to last st, k1.
ROW 6: [K1, drop yo] to last st, k1. This will elongate the stitches in the row below.
ROWS 7–8: Rep rows 1–2.
Rep rows 1–8 twice more, then rep rows 1 and 2 once more.

NEXT ROW (RS): Using the ssk cast-off method throughout, cast off 36 sts, knit until you have 126 (144, 162, 180, 198, 216, 234, 252) sts on right needle, cast off 72 sts, knit until you have 126 (144, 162, 180, 198, 216, 234, 252) sts on right needle, cast off remaining 36 sts to end. Break yarn and place live sts on holders or waste yarn.

BOTTOM EDGE

Work as for Top Edge, picking up along left edge of Lace Panel, working from cast-off edge to cast-on edge.

BLOCK WORK TO THE FOLLOWING DIMENSIONS:
35.5cm / 14" width x 187.5 (198.75, 206.25, 217.5, 225, 240, 251.25, 262.5)cm / 73¾ (78¼, 81¼, 85¾, 88½, 94½, 99, 103¼)"

JOIN
Using construction schematic as a reference, fold the strip of fabric as follows:
With WS up, fold right end under on the diagonal.
With WS up, fold left end under on the diagonal, working the fold close to the previous one.
Rotate work 135 degrees clockwise so that top edge of piece is now on the diagonal at the bottom right. Fold left end over, lining the edge up parallel with the diagonal on the bottom right. Rotate piece 135 degrees clockwise once more. The diagonal in the bottom right is now vertical on the left. Fold right end under to meet the edge of left end. Seam together.

This will arrange loop so that it creates a figure 8 (see construction schematic) with the seamed edge on top and in the centre. The cast-on and cast-off portions of the loop should meet up in the overlap; you may need to shift your figure 8 around slightly to ensure this but the cast-on and cast-offs should start and stop where the overlap begins.

With locking stitch markers or safety pins, pin the two layers of fabric together to hold them in place and aid with picking up stitches. Turn work over so that seam is now on the underside.

BORDER

Starting where noted on construction schematic, replace 63 (72, 81, 90, 99, 108, 117, 126) held sts on needle, PM, replace remaining 63 (72, 81, 90, 99, 108, 117, 126) held sts on needle to top edge of overlap point, PM, then, continuing to the right, replace 63 (72, 81, 90, 99, 108, 117, 126) held sts on needle, PM, replace remaining 63 (72, 81, 90, 99, 108, 117, 126) held sts on needle to bottom edge of overlap point. PM for beg of round and join to work in the round, being careful not to twist. *252 (288, 324, 360, 396, 432, 468, 504) sts*

ROUND 1: [K1, ssk, knit to marker, SM, knit to 3 sts before marker, k2tog, k1, SM] twice. *4 sts dec*
ROUND 2: Purl.
ROUND 3: [K1, yo, ssk, (yo, k1) to marker, yo, SM, (k1, yo) to 3 sts before marker, k2tog, yo, k1, SM] twice. *4 sts dec*
ROUND 4: [P1, drop yo] to 8 sts before marker, [p3, drop yo] twice, SM, [p3, drop yo] twice, [p1, drop yo] to marker, SM] twice. This will elongate the stitches in the row below. *8 sts inc*
ROUNDS 5–8: Rep rounds 1–2 twice.
Rep rounds 1–8 twice more.

Cast off all sts using modified Jeny's Surprisingly Stretchy cast-off as before.

RIGHT SLEEVE

Starting where noted on construction schematic, replace 126 (144, 162, 180, 198, 216, 234, 252) held sts on 40cm needle. Join to work in the round and PM for beg of round.

ROUND 1: Work round 1 of Lace Panel (in the round), working bracketed repeat a total of 7 (8, 9, 10, 11, 12, 13, 14) times.

Work even in pattern as est until round 12 of Lace Panel (in the round) is complete, then rep rounds 1–12 twice more.

DECREASE

Switch to your preferred method for small-circumference knitting when needed.

ROUND 1: [K2, k2tog, ssk, k2, p1, 1/3 RC, 1/3 LC, p1] to end. *112 (128, 144, 160, 176, 192, 208, 224) sts*
ROUND 2: [K6, p1, k8, p1] to end.
ROUND 3: [K1, k2tog, ssk, k1, p1, k1, 1/2 RC, 1/2 LC, k1, p1] to end. *98 (112, 126, 140, 154, 168, 182, 196) sts*
ROUND 4: [K4, p1, k8, p1] to end.
ROUND 5: [K2tog, ssk, p1, k2, k2tog, (yo) twice, ssk, k2, p1] to end. *84 (96, 108, 120, 132, 144, 156, 168) sts*
ROUND 6: [K2, p1, k3, (k1, p1) into double yo, k3, p1] to end.
ROUND 7: [K2, p1, k2, k2tog, ssk, k2, p1] to end. *70 (80, 90, 100, 110, 120, 130, 140) sts*
ROUND 8: [K2, p1, k6, p1] to end.
ROUND 9: [K2, p1, k1, k2tog, ssk, k1, p1] to end. *56 (64, 72, 80, 88, 96, 104, 112) sts*
ROUND 10: [K2, p1, k4, p1] to end.
ROUND 11: [K2, p1, k2tog, ssk, p1] to end. *42 (48, 54, 60, 66, 72, 78, 84) sts*
ROUND 12: [K2, p1] to end.

GARTER EDGING

ROUND 1: Knit.
ROUND 2: Purl.
ROUNDS 3–6: Rep rounds 1–2 twice more.
ROUND 7: [K1, yo] to last st, k1.
ROUND 8: [P1, drop yo] to last st, p1. This will elongate the stitches in the row below.
ROUNDS 9–14: Rep rounds 1–6.

Cast off all sts using modified Jeny's Surprisingly Stretchy cast-off.

Repeat for Left Sleeve.

FINISHING

Weave in all ends and block to measurements.

MIHARA SCHEMATIC KEY

A. Lace panel width: 35.5cm / 14" width
B. Elongated garter panel width: 6cm / 2½"
C. Panel length: 187.5 (198.75, 206.25, 217.5, 225, 240, 251.25, 262.5) cm / 73¾ (78¼, 81¼, 85¾, 88½, 94½, 99, 103¼)"
D. Back width after seaming: 47.5 (50.5, 52, 55, 57, 61, 63.5, 66.5)cm / 18¾ (19¾, 20½, 21¾, 22½, 24, 25, 26¼)"
E. Armhole circumference: 60 (68.5, 77, 85.5, 94.5, 103, 111.5, 120)cm / 23½ (27, 30¼, 33¾, 37, 40½, 43¾, 47¼)"
F. Cuff circumference: 20 (23, 25.5, 28.5, 31.5, 34.5, 37, 40)cm / 7¾ (9, 10, 11¼, 12½, 13½, 14½, 15¾)"
G. Border width: 5.5cm / 2¼"

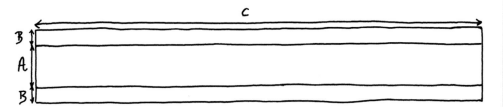

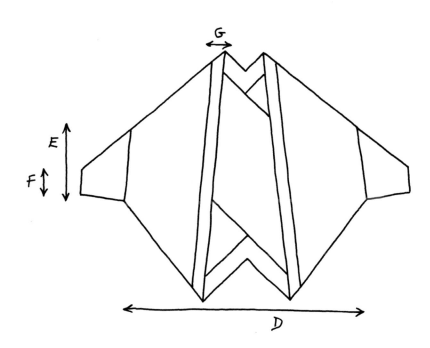

Twist: Mihara

Lace Panel (Flat)

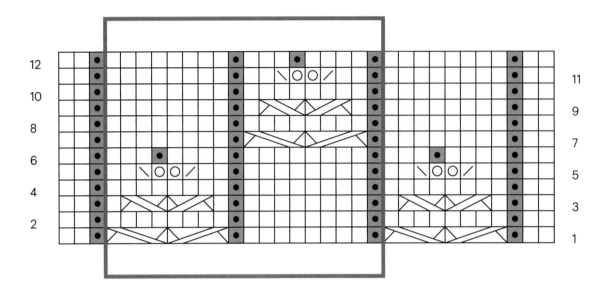

Lace Panel (In the Round)

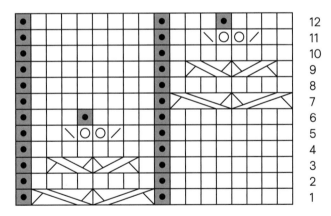

Sleeve Decreases

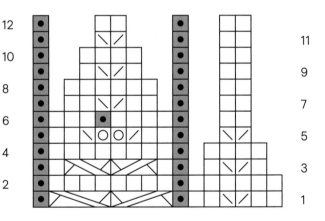

□	knit on RS, purl on WS		⬛ (1/2 RC symbol)	1/2 RC
⬛•	purl on RS, knit on WS		(1/2 LC symbol)	1/2 LC
╱	k2tog		(1/3 RC symbol)	1/3 RC
╲	ssk		(1/3 LC symbol)	1/3 LC
○	yo		⬛	repeat

Pleat:
Rei

Sometimes the simple ideas are the
most powerful. Taking the concept
of the knitted pleat, Rei juxtaposes
soft stocking stitch against dramatic
twisted-stitch lace to create a cowl
that swirls softly on your shoulders.

*Named after Rei Kawakubo, founder of the label Comme des Garçons,
known for her use of volume, pleating, and unexpected silhouettes.*

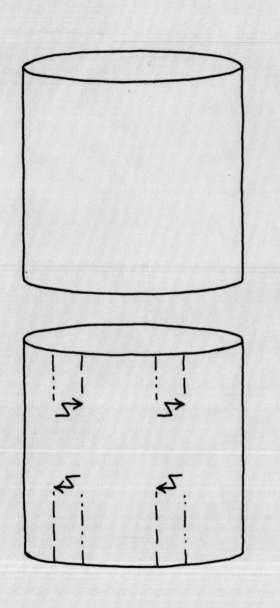

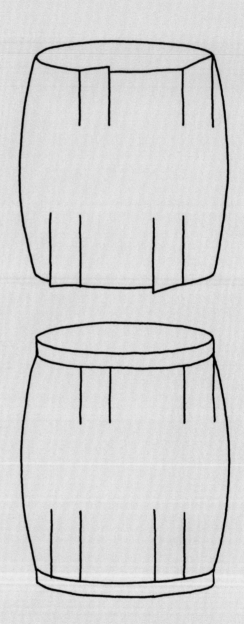

One size:

66.5cm / 26¾" circumference x
40.25cm / 16" deep

Yarn: Myak (pictured p73, p76)

Baby Yak | Silk (light fingering/4-ply
weight; 50% yak, 50% silk; 115m /
126yds per 25g skein)

Shade: Chanda; 4 skeins

OR

**Yarn: Amores Yarn Studio (pictured
p78, p79)**

Raíz (fingering/4-ply weight: 100%
superwash fine Merino; 398m / 435yds
per 100g skein)

Shade: Empire; 1 skein

Gauge:

25 sts & 35 rounds = 10cm / 4" over
stocking stitch on 3.75mm needles
after blocking.

15 sts & 16 rounds of Lace panel repeat =
6.5cm / 2½" wide x 5cm / 2" deep

Needles:

3.75mm / US 5 circular needle, 40cm /
16" length

Always use a needle size that will result
in the correct gauge after blocking.

Notions:

Crochet hook and scrap yarn for
provisional cast-on, 9 stitch markers,
tapestry needle, 2 DPNs in same size
as gauge needle

Notes:

Rei is started from the top down with a
provisional cast-on. After the body is
complete, pleats are worked along the
live stitches and the bottom hem is
finished with 1x1 twisted rib.
The provisional cast-on at the top edge
is unzipped and placed onto the needle,
and pleats are worked across these
stitches. Once this is complete, a few
rounds of garter stitch are worked and
then twisted rib completes the top edge.

Stitch Glossary:

1/1 LC: Sl 1 to cable needle, hold in
front, k1, k1 from cable needle.
1/1 RC: Sl 1 to cable needle, hold in
back, k1, k1 from cable needle.

CHARTS – WRITTEN INSTRUCTIONS

LACE PANEL

ROUND 1: K1tbl, yo, [k1tbl, p1] twice,
k1tbl, s2kpo, k1tbl, [p1, k1tbl] twice,
yo, k1tbl.
ROUND 2: [K1tbl, p1] 3 times, (k1tbl)
3 times, [p1, k1tbl] 3 times.
ROUND 3: K1tbl, yo, [p1, k1tbl] twice,
p1, s2kpo, p1, [k1tbl, p1] twice, yo, k1tbl.
ROUND 4: K1tbl, k1, [p1, k1tbl] 5 times,
p1, k1, k1tbl.
ROUNDS 5-8: Rep rounds 1-4.
ROUND 9: Ssk, [p1, k1tbl] twice, p1, yo,
k1tbl, yo, p1, [k1tbl, p1] twice, k2tog.
ROUND 10: [K1tbl, p1] 3 times, k1, k1tbl,
k1, [p1, k1tbl] 3 times.
ROUND 11: Ssk, [k1tbl, p1] twice, [k1tbl,
yo] twice, k1tb1, [p1, k1tbl] twice, k2tog.
ROUND 12: K1tbl, [k1tbl, p1] 6 times,
(k1tbl) twice.
ROUNDS 13-16: Rep rounds 9-12.

PATTERN BEGINS

Using scrap yarn and crochet hook,
provisionally cast on 180 sts. Join to work
in the round and PM for beg of round.

ROUND 1: [Work round 1 of Lace Panel,
PM, k30, PM] 3 times, work round 1 of
Lace Panel, PM, k30 to end.
ROUND 2: [Work next round of Lace
Panel, SM, knit to marker, SM] 3 times,
work next round of Lace Panel, SM,
knit to end.

Work even in pattern as est until
round 16 of Lace Panel is complete,
then rep rounds 1-16 of Lace Panel
a further 7 times.

BOTTOM PLEAT

SET-UP ROUND 1: Sl1, *[k1tbl, p1] to 2
sts before marker, k1tbl, sl 1, remove
marker, replace slipped st onto left
needle, 1/1 LC, PM, knit to 1 st before
next marker, PM, sl 1, remove marker,
replace slipped st onto left needle,
1/1 RC; rep from * to end. PM for new
beg of round. *17 sts in each Rib Panel;
28 sts in each St st panel*

SET-UP ROUND 2: *[K1tbl, p1] to 1 st
before marker, k1tbl, SM, k13, k2tog, k13,
SM; rep from * to end. *176 sts; 17 sts in
each Rib Panel; 27 sts in each St st panel*

PLEAT ROUND: *[K1tbl, p1] to 1 st
before marker, k1tbl, remove marker,
slip next 9 sts to first DPN (DPNA), slip
next 9 sts to second DPN (DPNB), turn
DPNB counterclockwise and parallel
to and in front of DPNA, bring left
working needle parallel to and in front
of DPNs, [insert right working needle
through the first st on left working
needle, then through first st on DPNB,
then through first st on DPNA and knit
together] 9 times, remove marker; rep
from * to end. *104 sts*

NEXT ROUND: [K1tbl, p1] to end.

Work even in rib as est for 3 more rounds.

Cast off all sts using a modified Jeny's Surprisingly Stretchy cast-off as follows: K1, *backwards-yo, k1, slip first 2 sts over third; rep from * to end.

TOP PLEAT

Unzip provisional cast-on and place all 180 sts on needle. Join to work in the round and PM for beg of round.

PLEAT ROUND: *Slip next 10 sts to first DPN (DPNA), slip next 10 sts to second DPN (DPNB), turn DPNB counterclockwise and parallel to and in front of DPNA, bring left working needle parallel to and in front of DPNs, [insert right working needle through the first st on left working needle, then through first st on DPNB, then through first st on DPNA and knit together] 10 times, k15; rep from * to end. *100 sts*

NEXT ROUND: Purl.
NEXT ROUND: Knit.

Rep these 2 rounds once more.

NEXT ROUND: [K1tbl, p1] to end.

Work even in rib as est for 3 more rounds.

Cast off all sts using a modified Jeny's Surprisingly Stretchy cast-off as before.

FINISHING

Weave in all ends and block to measurements.

REI SCHEMATIC KEY

A. Circumference before pleating: 74cm / 29¼"

B. Height without edging: 36.5cm / 14½"

C. Circumference after pleating: 66.5cm / 26¾"

D. Top edging: 2.5cm / 1"

E. Bottom edging: 1.25cm / ½"

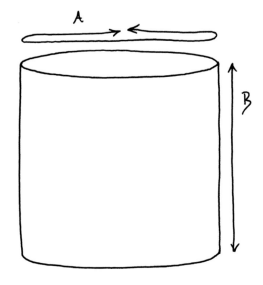

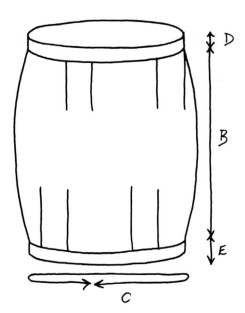

Lace Panel

ㅇ	ㅇ	•	ㅇ	•	ㅇ	•	•	•	ㅇ	•	ㅇ	•	ㅇ	ㅇ	16
/	ㅇ	•	ㅇ	•	ㅇ	O	ㅇ	O	ㅇ	•	ㅇ	•	ㅇ	\	15
ㅇ	•	ㅇ	•	ㅇ	•			•	ㅇ	•	ㅇ	•	ㅇ	ㅇ	14
/	•	ㅇ	•	ㅇ	O	ㅇ	O	•	ㅇ	•	ㅇ	•	ㅇ	\	13
ㅇ	ㅇ	•	ㅇ	•	ㅇ	•	ㅇ	•	ㅇ	•	ㅇ	•	ㅇ	ㅇ	12
/	ㅇ	•	ㅇ	•	ㅇ	O	ㅇ	O	ㅇ	•	ㅇ	•	ㅇ	\	11
ㅇ	•	ㅇ	•	ㅇ	•	ㅇ	•	ㅇ	•	ㅇ	•	ㅇ	•	ㅇ	10
/	•	ㅇ	•	ㅇ	O	ㅇ	O	ㅇ	•	ㅇ	•	ㅇ	•	\	9
ㅇ		•	ㅇ	•	ㅇ	•	ㅇ	•	ㅇ	•	ㅇ	•		ㅇ	8
ㅇ	O	•	ㅇ	•	ㅇ	•	⋀	•	ㅇ	•	ㅇ	•	O	ㅇ	7
ㅇ	•	ㅇ	•	ㅇ	•	ㅇ	ㅇ	ㅇ	•	ㅇ	•	ㅇ	•	ㅇ	6
ㅇ	O	ㅇ	•	ㅇ	•	ㅇ	⋀	ㅇ	•	ㅇ	•	ㅇ	O	ㅇ	5
ㅇ		•	ㅇ	•	ㅇ	•	ㅇ	•	ㅇ	•	ㅇ	•		ㅇ	4
ㅇ	O	•	ㅇ	•	ㅇ	•	⋀	•	ㅇ	•	ㅇ	•	O	ㅇ	3
ㅇ	•	ㅇ	•	ㅇ	•	ㅇ	ㅇ	ㅇ	•	ㅇ	•	ㅇ	•	ㅇ	2
ㅇ	O	ㅇ	•	ㅇ	•	ㅇ	⋀	ㅇ	•	ㅇ	•	ㅇ	O	ㅇ	1

☐	knit
ㅇ	ktbl
•	purl
/	k2tog
\	ssk
⋀	s2kpo
O	yo

Go For It: Yuko

Rotate, overlap, fold—Yuko is a personal challenge to think outside the box, to match graceful stitch patterns with divergent construction and gladsome making. Worked sideways, top down, and on the bias with textures, cables, and lace (not usually all at the same time), Yuko is joy in knitted form and a reimagining of Callas, a shrug design by Bristol, originally published in Pom Pom Quarterly Issue 15, Winter 2015.

Named after Yuko Nishimura, a contemporary artist who uses origami to create complex and contoured architecture out of paper.

Sizes:

1 (2, 3, 4, 5, 6, 7, 8)

Finished back width:

85 (90, 92, 94.5, 97, 102, 104, 106.5)cm / 33½ (35¼, 36¼, 37¼, 38¼, 40, 41, 42)" – to fit 76-86 (86.5-96, 96.5-106, 106.5-116, 116.5-126, 126.5-136, 136.5-146, 146.5-156)cm / 30-33¾ (34-37¾, 38-41¾, 42-45¾, 46-49½, 49¾-53½, 53¾-57½, 57¾-61½)" bust circumference

Model has 127cm / 50" bust, stands 175cm / 5'9" tall, and is wearing size 5.

Yarn: Kettle Yarn Co. (pictured p81, p95, p98)

Beyul DK (DK weight, superwash Merino, yak, silk; 212m / 232yds per 100g skein)

Shade: Black Quartz; 4 (5, 5, 6, 6, 7, 7, 8) skeins

OR

Yarn: Ocean by the Sea (pictured p96, p97, p99)

BFL Roving (DK weight, 100% Bluefaced Leicester; 200m / 218yds per 100g skein)

Shade: Heather, I Blush; 5 (5, 6, 6, 7, 7, 8, 8) skeins

Gauge:

24 sts & 36 rows = 10cm / 4" over 2x2 garter rib on 4mm needles after blocking.

25.5 sts & 32 rows = 10cm / 4" over stocking stitch on 4mm needles after blocking.

Needles:

4mm / US 6 circular needle, 80cm / 32" length, or straight needles

4mm / US 6 circular needle, 40cm / 16" length

Always use a needle size that will result in the correct gauge after blocking.

Notions:

Cable needle, 1 stitch marker, 2 locking stitch markers, tapestry needle

Notes:

Yuko starts with two front bands knit separately and seamed together at the end to form a V shape. From the bottom edge of that V, stitches are picked up and knit down in a chevron to create the body of the shrug. Next, half of those stitches are put on hold and the other half are worked sideways, decreasing quickly to create a triangle. The other side is worked the same way, and these triangles are seamed to the edges of the front bands to create the armholes. The armholes are then finished with a stretchy cast-off to prevent curling. When Right and Left parts of the garment are referred to, they are the wearer's right and left.

Stitch Glossary:

3/3 LC: Sl 3 to cable needle, hold in front, k3, k3 from cable needle.
3/3 RC: Sl 3 to cable needle, hold in back, k3, k3 from cable needle.

2X2 GARTER RIB (FLAT)
ROW 1 (RS): Knit.
ROW 2 (WS): P2, [k2, p2] to end.
Rep rows 1-2 for pattern.

PATTERN BEGINS

RIGHT FRONT BAND

Using the long-tail method and longer needles, cast on 3 sts.
NEXT ROW (WS): Purl.

INCREASE SECTION SET-UP
ROW 1 (RS): Sl1wyib, M1L, k2. *4 sts*
ROW 2 (WS): P2, k1, p1.
ROW 3: Sl1wyib, knit to last 2 sts, M1L, k2. *1 sts inc*
ROW 4: P3, k1, p1.
ROW 5: Rep row 3. *6 sts*
ROW 6: P4, k1, p1.
ROW 7: Rep row 3. *7 sts*
ROW 8: [P2, k1] twice, p1.

RIB SET-UP
ROW 1 (RS): Sl1wyib, knit to last 2 sts, M1L, k2. *1 st inc*
ROW 2 (WS): P2, k1, [k1, p2, k1] to last st, p1.
ROW 3: Rep row 1. *1 st inc*
ROW 4: P3, k1, [k1, p2, k1] to last st, p1.
ROW 5: Rep row 1. *1 st inc*
ROW 6: P4, k1, [k1, p2, k1] to last st, p1.
ROW 7: Rep row 1. *1 st inc*
ROW 8: P2, [k1, p2, k1] to last st, p1.

Rep rows 1-8 of Rib Set-Up a further 4 times. *27 sts*

CABLE AND LACE SET-UP
ROW 1 (RS): Sl1wyib, knit to last 2 sts, yo, k2. *28 sts*
ROW 2 (WS): P3, [k1, p2, k1] to last st, p1.
ROW 3: Rep row 1. *29 sts*
ROW 4: P3, k1, [k1, p2, k1] to last st, p1.
ROW 5: Rep row 1. *30 sts*
ROW 6: P4, k1, [k1, p2, k1] to last st, p1.
ROW 7: Rep row 1. *31 sts*
ROW 8: P5, k1, [k1, p2, k1] to last st, p1.
ROW 9: Rep row 1. *32 sts*
ROW 10: P6, k1, [k1, p2, k1] to last st, p1.
ROW 11: Rep row 1. *33 sts*
ROW 12: P7, k1, [k1, p2, k1] to last st, p1.
ROW 13: Rep row 1. *34 sts*
ROW 14: P8, k1, [k1, p2, k1] to last st, p1.
ROW 15: Rep row 1. *35 sts*

ROW 16: P9, k1, [k1, p2, k1] to last st, p1.
ROW 17: Rep row 1. *36 sts*
ROW 18: P10, k1, [k1, p2, k1] to last st, p1.
ROW 19: Rep row 1. *37 sts*
ROW 20: P11, k1, [k1, p2, k1] to last st, p1.
ROW 21: Rep row 1. *38 sts*
ROW 22: P12, k1, [k1, p2, k1] to last st, p1.
ROW 23: Sl1wyib, knit to last 8 sts, k2tog, k2, [yo, k1] twice, yo, k2. *40 sts*
ROW 24: P9, p2tog, p3, k1, [k1, p2, k1] to last st, p1. *39 sts*
ROW 25: Sl1wyib, knit to last 11 sts, k2tog, k3, [yo, k1] twice, k2, yo, k2. *41 sts*
ROW 26: P12, p2tog, p1, k1, [k1, p2, k1] to last st, p1. *40 sts*
ROW 27: Sl1wyib, knit to last 6 sts, k2tog, [yo, k1] twice, yo, k2. *42 sts*
ROW 28: P7, p2tog, p7, k1, [k1, p2, k1] to last st, p1. *41 sts*
ROW 29: Sl1wyib, knit to last 9 sts, k2tog, [k1, yo] twice, k3, yo, k2. *43 sts*
ROW 30: P10, p2tog, p5, k1, [k1, p2, k1] to last st, p1. *42 sts*
ROW 31: Sl1wyib, knit to last 12 sts, k2tog, k2, [yo, k1] twice, k4, yo, k2. *44 sts*
ROW 32: P13, p2tog, p3, k1, [k1, p2, k1] to last st, p1. *43 sts*
ROW 33: Sl1wyib, knit to last 15 sts, k2tog, k3, [yo, k1] twice, k6, yo, k2. *45 sts*
ROW 34: P16, p2tog, p1, k1, [k1, p2, k1] to last st, p1. *44 sts*
Place locking stitch marker at left edge of fabric as seen from RS to aid with picking up stitches and seaming later.

BAND REPEAT
ROW 1 (RS): Sl1wyib, k33, k2tog, yo, k1, yo, 3/3 LC, k1. *1 st inc*
ROW 2 (WS): P10, p2tog, p7, k1, [k1, p2, k1] to last st, p1. *1 st dec*
ROW 3: Sl1wyib, k31, k2tog, [k1, yo] twice, k8. *1 st inc*
ROW 4: P12, p2tog, p5, k1, [k1, p2, k1] to last st, p1. *1 st dec*
ROW 5: Sl1wyib, k29, k2tog, k2, [yo, k1] twice, k8. *1 st inc*
ROW 6: P14, p2tog, p3, k1, [k1, p2, k1] to last st, p1. *1 st dec*
ROW 7: Sl1wyib, k27, k2tog, k3, [yo, k1] twice, k9. *1 st inc*

ROW 8: P16, p2tog, p1, k1, [k1, p2, k1] to last st, p1. *1 st dec*

Rep rows 1–8 of Band Repeat a further 7 (8, 9, 10, 11, 12, 13, 14) times.

RIB DECREASE
ROW 1 (RS): Sl1wyib, ssk, knit to last 10 sts, k2tog, yo, k1, yo, 3/3 LC, k1.
ROW 2 (WS): P10, p2tog, p7, k1, [k1, p2, k1] to last 4 sts, k1, p3. *1 st dec*
ROW 3: Sl1wyib, ssk, knit to last 12 sts, k2tog, [k1, yo] twice, k8.
ROW 4: P12, p2tog, p5, k1, [k1, p2, k1] to last 3 sts, k1, p2. *1 st dec*
ROW 5: Sl1wyib, ssk, knit to last 14 sts, k2tog, k2, [yo, k1] twice, k8.
ROW 6: P14, p2tog, p3, k1, [k1, p2, k1] to last 2 sts, k1, p1. *1 st dec*
ROW 7: Sl1wyib, ssk, knit to last 16 sts, k2tog, k3, [yo, k1] twice, k9.
ROW 8: P16, p2tog, p1, k1, [k1, p2, k1] to last st, p1. *1 st dec*

Rep rows 1–8 of Rib Decrease a further 3 times. *28 sts*

CABLE AND LACE DECREASE
ROW 1 (RS): Sl1wyib, ssk, knit to last 10 sts, k2tog, yo, k1, yo, 3/3 LC, k1.
ROW 2 (WS): P10, p2tog, p7, [k2, p2] twice, p1. *27 sts*
ROW 3: Sl1wyib, ssk, knit to last 12 sts, k2tog, [k1, yo] twice, k8.
ROW 4: P12, p2tog, p5, [k2, p2] twice. *26 sts*
ROW 5: Sl1wyib, ssk, knit to last 14 sts, k2tog, k2, [yo, k1] twice, k8.
ROW 6: P14, p2tog, p3, k2, p2, k2, p1. *25 sts*
ROW 7: Sl1wyib, ssk, knit to last 16 sts, k2tog, k3, [yo, k1] twice, k9.
ROW 8: P16, p2tog, p1, k2, p2, k1, p1. *24 sts*
ROW 9: Rep row 1.
ROW 10: P10, p2tog, p7, k2, p3. *23 sts*
ROW 11: Rep row 3.
ROW 12: P12, p2tog, p5, k2, p2. *22 sts*
ROW 13: Rep row 5.
ROW 14: P14, p2tog, p3, k1, p2. *21 sts*
ROW 15: Rep row 7.
ROW 16: P16, p2tog, p1, k1, p1. *20 sts*

ROW 17: Rep row 1.
ROW 18: P10, p2tog, p8. *19 sts*
ROW 19: Rep row 3.
ROW 20: P12, p2tog, p5. *18 sts*
ROW 21: Sl1wyib, ssk, knit to end. *1 st dec*
ROW 22: Purl.
ROWS 23–24: Rep rows 21–22. *16 sts*
ROW 25: Rep row 1.
ROW 26: P10, p2tog, p4. *15 sts*
ROWS 27–32: Rep rows 21 and 22 a further 3 times. *12 sts*
ROW 33: Sl1wyib, ssk, k2, 3/3 LC, k1. *11 sts*
ROW 34: Purl.
ROWS 36–50: Rep rows 21–22 a further 8 times. *3 sts*

Cast off all sts knitwise.

LEFT FRONT BAND

Using the long-tail method and larger needles, cast on 3 sts.
NEXT ROW (WS): Purl.

INCREASE SECTION SET-UP
ROW 1 (RS): K2, M1R, k1. *4 sts*
ROW 2 (WS): Sl1wyif, k1, p2.
ROW 3: K2, M1R, knit to end. *1 st inc*
ROW 4: Sl1wyif, k1, p3.
ROW 5: Rep row 3. *6 sts*
ROW 6: Sl1wyif, k1, p4.
ROW 7: Rep row 3. *7 sts*
ROW 8: Sl1wyif, [k1, p2] twice.

RIB SET-UP
ROW 1 (RS): K2, M1R, knit to end. *1 st inc*
ROW 2 (WS): Sl1wyif, [k1, p2, k1] to last 3 sts, k1, p2.
ROW 3: Rep row 1. *9 sts*
ROW 4: Sl1wyif, [k1, p2, k1] to last 4 sts, k1, p3.
ROW 5: Rep row 1. *10 sts*
ROW 6: Sl1wyif, [k1, p2, k1] to last 5 sts, k1, p4.
ROW 7: Rep row 1. *11 sts*
ROW 8: Sl1wyif, [k1, p2, k1] to last 2 sts, p2.

Rep rows 1–8 of Rib Set-Up a further 4 times. *27 sts*

CABLE AND LACE SET-UP
ROW 1 (RS): K2, yo, knit to end. *1 st inc*
ROW 2 (WS): Sl1wyif, [k1, p2, k1] to last 3 sts, p3.
ROW 3: Rep row 1. *29 sts*
ROW 4: Sl1wyif, [k1, p2, k1] to last 4 sts, k1, p3.
ROW 5: Rep row 1. *30 sts*
ROW 6: Sl1wyif, [k1, p2, k1] to last 5 sts, k1, p4.
ROW 7: Rep row 1. *31 sts*
ROW 8: Sl1wyif, [k1, p2, k1] to last 6 sts, k1, p5.
ROW 9: Rep row 1. *32 sts*
ROW 10: Sl1wyif, [k1, p2, k1] to last 7 sts, k1, p6.
ROW 11: Rep row 1. *33 sts*
ROW 12: Sl1wyif, [k1, p2, k1] to last 8 sts, k1, p7.
ROW 13: Rep row 1. *34 sts*
ROW 14: Sl1wyif, [k1, p2, k1] to last 9 sts, k1, p8.
ROW 15: Rep row 1. *35 sts*
ROW 16: Sl1wyif, [k1, p2, k1] to last 10 sts, k1, p9.
ROW 17: Rep row 1. *36 sts*
ROW 18: Sl1wyif, [k1, p2, k1] to last 11 sts, k1, p10.
ROW 19: Rep row 1. *37 sts*
ROW 20: Sl1wyif, [k1, p2, k1] to last 12 sts, k1, p11.
ROW 21: Rep row 1. *38 sts*
ROW 22: Sl1wyif, [k1, p2, k1] to last 13 sts, k1, p12.
ROW 23: K2, [yo, k1] 3 times, k1, ssk, knit to end. *40 sts*
ROW 24: Sl1wyif, [k1, p2, k1] to last 15 sts, k1, p3, ssp, p9. *39 sts*
ROW 25: K2, yo, k3, [yo, k1] twice, k3, ssk, knit to end. *41 sts*
ROW 26: Sl1wyif, [k1, p2, k1] to last 16 sts, k1, p1, ssp, p12. *40 sts*
ROW 27: K2, [yo, k1] twice, yo, ssk, knit to end. *42 sts*
ROW 28: Sl1wyif, [k1, p2, k1] to last 17 sts, k1, p7, ssp, p7. *41 sts*
ROW 29: K2, yo, k3, [yo, k1] twice, ssk, knit to end. *43 sts*
ROW 30: Sl1wyif, [k1, p2, k1] to last 18 sts, k1, p5, ssp, p10. *42 sts*
ROW 31: K2, yo, k5, [yo, k1] twice, k1, ssk, knit to end. *44 sts*
ROW 32: Sl1wyif, [k1, p2, k1] to last 19 sts, k1, p3, ssp, p13. *43 sts*
ROW 33: K2, yo, k7, [yo, k1] twice, k2, ssk, knit to end. *45 sts*
ROW 34: Sl1wyif, [k1, p2, k1] to last 20 sts, k1, p1, ssp, p16. *44 sts*

Place locking stitch marker at right edge of fabric as seen from RS to aid with picking up stitches and seaming later.

BAND REPEAT
ROW 1 (RS): K1, 3/3 RC, yo, k1, yo, ssk, knit to end. *1 st inc*
ROW 2 (WS): Sl1wyif, [k1, p2, k1] to last 20 sts, k1, p7, ssp, p10. *1 st dec*
ROW 3: K8, [yo, k1] twice, ssk, knit to end. *1 st inc*
ROW 4: Sl1wyif, [k1, p2, k1] to last 20 sts, k1, p5, ssp, p12. *1 st dec*
ROW 5: K9, [yo, k1] twice, k1, ssk, knit to end. *1 st inc*
ROW 6: Sl1wyif, [k1, p2, k1] to last 20 sts, k1, p3, ssp, p14. *1 st dec*
ROW 7: K10, [yo, k1] twice, k2, ssk, knit to end. *1 st inc*
ROW 8: Sl1wyif, [k1, p2, k1] to last 20 sts, k1, p1, ssp, p16. *1 st dec*

Rep rows 1–8 of Band Repeat a further 7 (8, 9, 10, 11, 12, 13, 14) times.

RIB DECREASE
ROW 1 (RS): K1, 3/3 RC, yo, k1, yo, ssk, knit to last 3 sts, k2tog, k1.
ROW 2 (WS): Sl1wyif, p2, k1, [k1, p2, k1] to last 20 sts, k1, p7, ssp, p10. *1 st dec*
ROW 3: K8, [yo, k1] twice, ssk, knit to last 3 sts, k2tog, k1.
ROW 4: Sl1wyif, p1, k1, [k1, p2, k1] to last 20 sts, k1, p5, ssp, p12. *1 st dec*
ROW 5: K9, [yo, k1] twice, k1, ssk, knit to last 3 sts, k2tog, k1.
ROW 6: Sl1wyif, k1, [k1, p2, k1] to last 20 sts, k1, p3, ssp, p14. *1 st dec*
ROW 7: K10, [yo, k1] twice, k2, ssk, knit to last 3 sts, k2tog, k1.
ROW 8: Sl1wyif, [k1, p2, k1] to last 20 sts, k1, p1, ssp, p16. *1 st dec*

Rep rows 1–8 of Rib Decrease a further 3 times. *28 sts*

CABLE AND LACE DECREASE
ROW 1 (RS): K1, 3/3 RC, yo, k1, yo, ssk, knit to last 3 sts, k2tog, k1.
ROW 2 (WS): Sl1wyif, [p2, k2] twice, p7, ssp, p10. *27 sts*
ROW 3: K8, [yo, k1] twice, ssk, knit to last 3 sts, k2tog, k1.
ROW 4: Sl1wyif, p1, k2, p2, k2, p5, ssp, p12. *26 sts*
ROW 5: K9, [yo, k1] twice, k1, ssk, knit to last 3 sts, k2tog, k1.
ROW 6: Sl1wyif, [k2, p2] twice, p1, ssp, p14. *25 sts*
ROW 7: K10, [yo, k1] twice, k2, ssk, knit to last 3 sts, k2tog, k1.
ROW 8: Sl1wyif, k1, p2, k2, p1, ssp, p16. *24 sts*
ROW 9: Rep row 1.
ROW 10: Sl1wyif, p2, k2, p7, ssp, p10. *23 sts*
ROW 11: Rep row 3.
ROW 12: Sl1wyif, p1, k2, p5, ssp, p12. *22 sts*
ROW 13: Rep row 5.
ROW 14: Sl1wyif, p1, k1, p3, ssp, p14. *21 sts*
ROW 15: Rep row 7.
ROW 16: Sl1wyif, k1, p1, ssp, p16. *20 sts*
ROW 17: Rep row 1.
ROW 18: Sl1wyif, p7, ssp, p10. *19 sts*
ROW 19: Rep row 3.
ROW 20: Sl1wyif, p4, ssp, p12. *18 sts*
ROW 21: Knit to last 3 sts, k2tog, k1. *1 st dec*
ROW 22: Sl1wyif, purl to end.
ROWS 23–24: Rep rows 21–22. *16 sts*
ROW 25: Rep row 1.
ROW 26: Sl1wyif, p3, ssp, purl to end. *15 sts*
ROWS 27–32: Rep rows 21–22 a further 3 times. *12 sts*
ROW 33: K1, 3/3 RC, k2, k2tog, k1. *11 sts*
ROW 34: Sl1wyif, purl to end.
ROWS 35–50: Rep rows 21–22 a further 8 times. *3 sts*

Cast off all sts knitwise.
With RS facing and using mattress stitch, seam together decrease edge of Left and Right Front Bands.

BODY

Starting at locking stitch marker on the Left Front Band, and moving towards the seam along the cabled edge of the Left Front Band, pick up and knit 142 (146, 150, 158, 162, 166, 170, 178) sts in edge of Left Front Band to seam, PM, then pick up and knit 142 (146, 150, 158, 162, 166, 170, 178) sts in cabled edge of Right Front Band to locking stitch marker on the Right Front Band. *284 (292, 300, 316, 324, 332, 340, 356) sts*

NEXT ROW (WS): Purl.

ROW 1 (RS): K1, k2tog, knit to 1 st before marker, M1L, k1, SM, k1, M1R, knit to last 3 sts, ssk, k1.
ROW 2 (WS): Purl.

Work as est until work measures 19.75 (19.75, 21.5, 23.5, 25.5, 25.5, 26.75, 28.5)cm / 7¾ (7¾, 8½, 9¼, 10, 10, 10½, 11¼)" from pick up along edge, ending after a WS row. With RS facing, place all sts after the marker on st holder or waste yarn. *142 (146, 150, 158, 162, 166, 170, 178) sts on needle*

LEFT BODY TRIANGLE

ROW 1 (RS): Sl1wyib, knit to last 3 sts, k2tog, k1. *1 st dec*
ROW 2 (WS): P1, p2tog, p2, [k2, p2] to end. *1 st dec*
ROW 3: Rep row 1. *1 st dec*
ROW 4: P1, p2tog, [k2, p2] to end. *1 st dec*

Rep rows 1-4 a further 32 (33, 34, 36, 37, 38, 39, 41) times. *10 sts*

LEFT BODY TRIANGLE FINISH

ROW 1 (RS): Sl1wyib, knit to last 3 sts, k2tog, k1. *1 st dec*
ROW 2 (WS): P1, p2tog, p2, k2, p2. *8 sts*
ROW 3: Rep row 1. *7 sts*
ROW 4: P1, p2tog, k2, p2. *6 sts*
ROW 5: Rep row 1. *5 sts*
ROW 6: P1, p2tog, p2. *4 sts*
ROW 7: Rep row 1. *3 sts*
ROW 8: P1, p2tog. *2 sts*
ROW 9: K2tog. *1 st*

Break yarn and pull through remaining st.

RIGHT BODY TRIANGLE

Return held 142 (146, 150, 158, 162, 166, 170, 178) sts to needle, ready to work a RS row.

ROW 1 (RS): K1, ssk, knit to end. *1 st dec*
ROW 2 (WS): Sl1wyif, p1, [k2, p2] to last 3 sts, ssp, p1. *1 st dec*
ROW 3: Rep row 1. *1 st dec*
ROW 4: Sl1wyif, p1, [k2, p2] to last 5 sts, k2, ssp, p1. *1 st dec*

Rep rows 1-4 a further 32 (33, 34, 36, 37, 38, 39, 41) times. *10 sts*

RIGHT BODY TRIANGLE FINISH

ROW 1 (RS): K1, ssk, knit to end. *1 st dec*
ROW 2 (WS): Sl1wyif, p1, k2, p2, ssp, p1. *8 sts*
ROW 3: Rep row 1. *7 sts*
ROW 4: Sl1wyif, p1, k2, ssp, p1. *6 sts*
ROW 5: Rep row 1. *5 sts*
ROW 6: Sl1wyif, p1, ssp, p1. *4 sts*
ROW 7: Rep row 1. *3 sts*
ROW 8: Ssp, p1. *2 sts*
ROW 9: Ssk. *1 st*

Break yarn and pull through remaining st.

FINISHING

Block piece to schematic measurements. Starting at point of Right Body Triangle and point of Right Band cast-on, seam pieces together, ending at locking stitch marker. Leave marker in place to aid with armhole finishing. Repeat for Left Body Triangle and Left Band cast-on.

RIGHT ARMHOLE FINISHING

With shorter circular needle and starting at locking stitch marker, pick up and knit 3 sts for every 4 rows around edge. Stitch count should be approximately 91 (94, 101, 112, 119, 122, 128, 139) sts. Join to work in the round and PM for beg of round.

NEXT ROUND: Knit.
NEXT ROUND: Cast off all sts using a purl modified Jeny's Surprisingly Stretchy cast-off as follows: P1, *backwards-yo, p1, slip first 2 sts over third; rep from * to end.

Repeat for Left Armhole Finishing. Weave in all ends and steam-block seams.

YUKO SCHEMATIC KEY

A. Front band width: 18.5cm / 7¼"
B. Front band length: 45.5 (48, 50.5, 53, 55.5, 58, 60.5, 63)cm / 17¾ (18¾, 19¾, 20¾, 21¾, 22¾, 23¾, 24¾)"
C. Front band depth at front edge: 31.5cm / 12½"
D. Back width: 78 (81, 83, 88, 90, 92, 94, 99)cm / 31 (32, 33, 34½, 35½, 36, 37, 39)"
E. Chevron depth: 19.75 (19.75, 21.5, 23.5, 25.5, 25.5, 26.75, 28.5)cm / 7¾ (7¾, 8½, 9¼, 10, 10, 10½, 11¼)"
F. Body triangle width: 55.5 (57.5, 59, 62, 63.5, 65, 66.5, 70)cm / 22 (22½, 23¼, 24½, 25, 25¾, 26¼, 27½)"
G. Body triangle length: 41.5 (42.5, 44, 46.5, 47.5, 49, 50, 52.5)cm / 16¼ (16¾, 17¼, 18¼, 18¾, 19¼, 19¾, 20¾)"
H. Body triangle depth: 21 (21.5, 22, 23.5, 24, 24.5, 25, 26.5)cm / 8¼ (8½, 8¾, 9¼ 9½, 9¾, 10, 10½)"
I. Armhole circumference: 35.5 (37, 39.5, 44, 46.5, 48, 50, 54.5)cm / 14 (14½, 15½, 17¼, 18¼, 18¾, 19¾, 21½)"
J. Seam length: 38 (39, 39.5, 40, 40.5, 41, 41.5, 43)cm / 15 (15¼, 15½, 16, 16, 16½, 16½, 16¾)"
K. Shoulder: 32.5 (32.5, 33.5, 35, 36.5, 36.5, 37.5, 38.5)cm / 12¾ (12¾, 13¼, 13¾, 14¼, 14¼, 14¾, 15¼)"

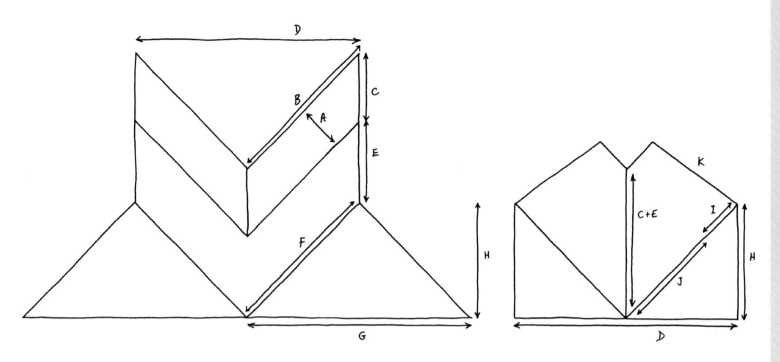

Right Increase Section Set-Up

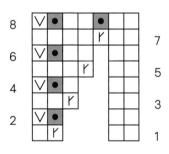

Left Increase Section Set-Up

Right Rib Set-Up

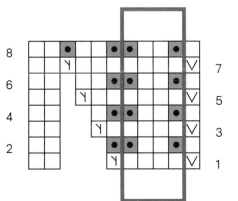

Left Rib Set-Up

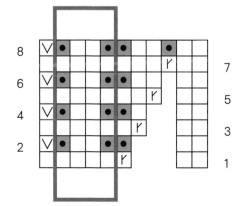

Right Cable and Lace Set-Up

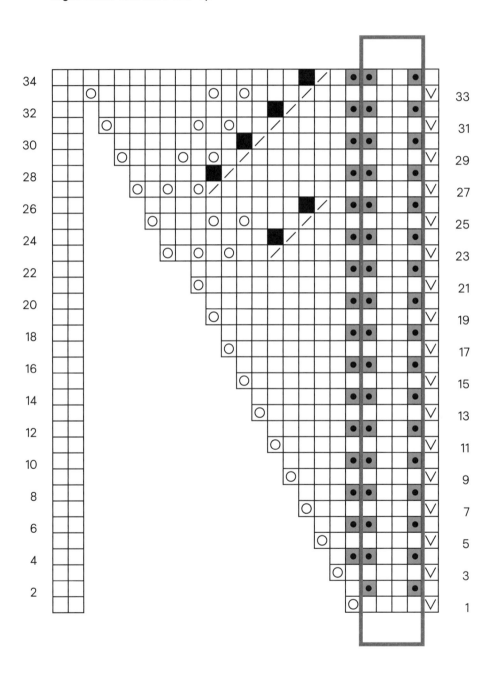

Left Cable and Lace Set-Up

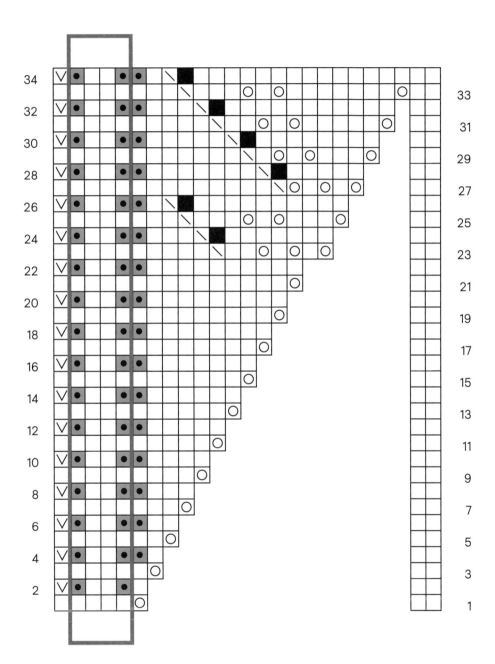

Right Band Repeat

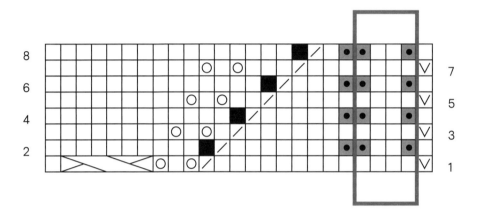

Right Rib Decrease

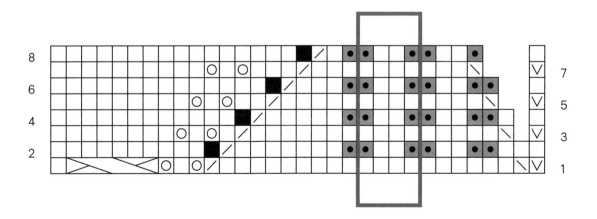

Left Band Repeat

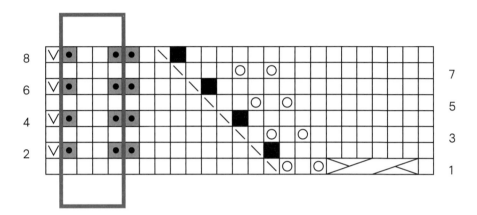

Left Rib Decrease

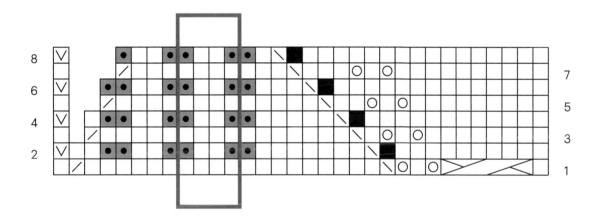

Right Cable and Lace Decrease

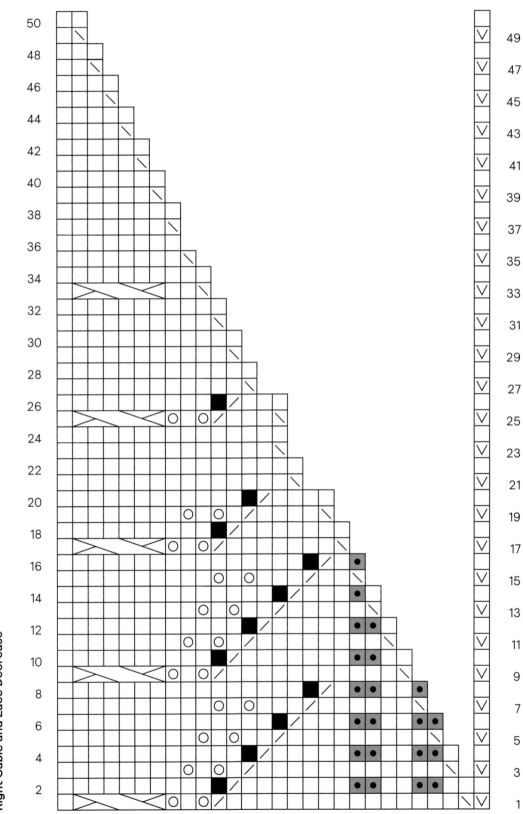

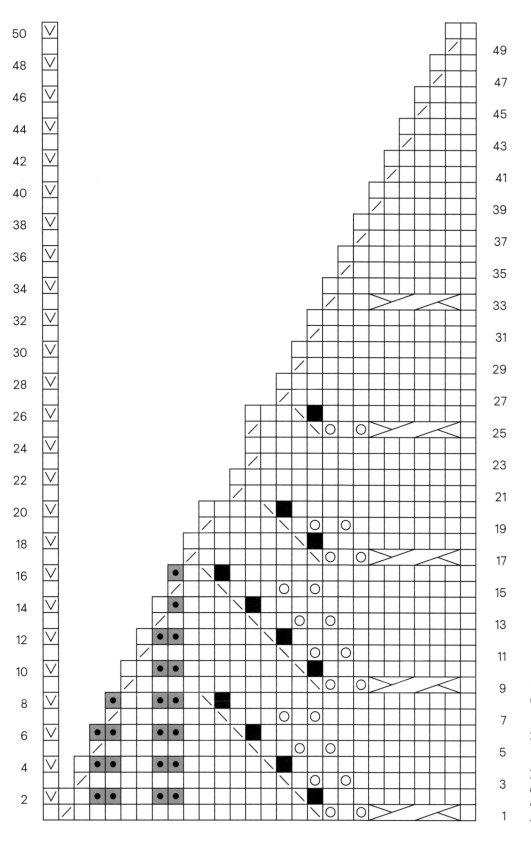

Left Cable and Lace Decrease

Left Body Triangle

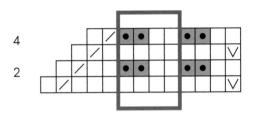

Right Body Triangle

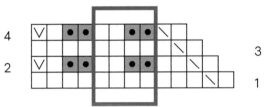

Left Body Triangle Finish

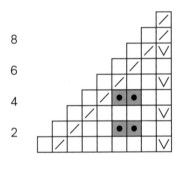

Right Body Triangle Finish

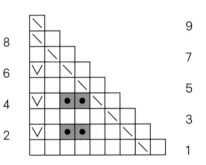

☐	knit on RS, purl on WS
☐(o)	purl on RS, knit on RS
╱	k2tog on RS, p2tog on WS
╲	ssk on RS, ssp on WS
Ɣ	M1R
⅄	M1L

Ⓞ	yo
ⱽ	sl1wyib on RS, sl1wyif on WS
■	no stitch
⧓	3/3 LC
⧓	3/3 RC
☐	repeat

Yarn Support

Amores Yarn Studio
Raíz
amoresyarnstudio.shop

CoopKnits
Socks Yeah!
coopknits.co.uk

John Arbon Textiles
Alpaca Supreme (swatches)
jarbon.com

Kettle Yarn Co.
Beyul DK
kettleyarnco.co.uk

La Bien Aimée
Merino DK
labienaimee.com

Moel View Yarn
Infallible DK
moelviewyarn.com

Myak
Baby Yak | Silk
myak.it

Neighborhood Fiber Co.
Studio DK
neighborhoodfiberco.com

North Light Fibers
Water Street
northlightfibers.com

Ocean by the Sea
BFL Roving
etsy.com/uk/shop/Oceanbythesea

Stolen Stitches
Nua
stolenstitches.com

The Farmer's Daughter Fibers
Pishkun
thefarmersdaughterfibers.com

Three Fates
Eponymous
three-fates-yarn.myshopify.com

Abbreviations

1/1 LC	Sl 1 to cable needle, hold in front, k1, k1 from cable needle	**beg**	Beginning
1/1 RC	Sl 1 to cable needle, hold in back, k1, k1 from cable needle	**brk**	Knit slipped stitch and yo together
1/1 LPT	Sl 1 to cable needle, hold in front, p1, k1tbl from cable needle	**brkyobrk**	K1, keeping brk on left needle, yo around right needle, knit into brk once more and drop from left needle
1/1 RPT	Sl 1 to cable needle, hold in back, k1tbl, p1 from cable needle	**brkyobrkyobrk**	*K1, keeping brk on left needle, yo around right needle; rep from * once, knit into brk once more and drop from left needle
1/1/1 LPT	Sl 1 to cable needle, hold in front, slip next st to a second cable needle and hold in back, k1tbl, p1 from back cable needle, k1tbl from front cable needle	**brp**	Purl slipped st and yo together
		cable cast-on	Insert right needle between first and second sts on left needle. Wrap yarn and pull through as if knitting. Do not slip sts from left needle. Place new stitch over left needle (1 stitch cast on). Repeat as directed by pattern
1/2 LC	Sl 1 to cable needle, hold in front, k2, k1 from cable needle		
1/2 RC	Sl 2 to cable needle, hold in back, k1, k2 from cable needle		
1/2 LPT	Sl 1 to cable needle, hold in front, p2, k1tbl from cable needle	**cast off**	Bind off
		dec	Decrease(d)
1/2 RPT	Sl 2 to cable needle, hold in back, k1tbl, p2 from cable needle	**dec-4**	Slip 1 knit column as if to knit, slip next 2 columns together as if to knit, k1, pass 2 columns over, return stitch to left needle, pass next column over, return stitch to right needle, pass slipped column over
1/3 LC	Sl 1 to cable needle, hold in front, k3, k1 from cable needle		
1/3 RC	Sl 3 to cable needle, hold in back, k1, k3 from cable needle		
2/3 LC	Sl 2 to cable needle, hold in front, k3, k2 from cable needle	**DPN(s)**	Double-pointed needle(s)
		est	Established
2/3 RC	Sl 3 to cable needle, hold in back, k2, k3 from cable needle	**inc**	Increase(d)
		k	Knit
3/3 LC	Sl 3 to cable needle, hold in front, k3, k3 from cable needle	**k1tbl**	Knit 1 stitch through the back loop
		k2tog	Knit 2 stitches together
3/3 RC	Sl 3 to cable needle, hold in back, k3, k3 from cable needle	**k2togtbl**	Knit 2 stitches together through the back loops
		kfb	Knit into the front and back of the next stitch
backwards-yo	Move yarn to front of work, then round the needle to the back	**M**	Marker
		M1L	Make 1 Left; pick up strand between the two needles from the front to back with the tip of left needle, knit into the back of this stitch

M1P	Make 1 Purlwise; pick up strand between the two needles from the front to the back with the tip of left needle, purl this stitch through the back loop
M1R	Make 1 Right; pick up strand between the two needles from back to front with the tip of left needle, knit into the front of this stitch
p	Purl
p1tbl	Purl 1 stitch through the back loop
p2tog	Purl 2 stitches together
p2togtbl	Purl 2 stitches together through the back loop
pfb	Purl into the front and back of the next stitch
PM	Place marker
REM	Remain(ing)
rep	Repeat
RS	Right side(s)
s2kpo	Slip 2 stitches together knitwise, k1, pass slipped stitches over
sl	Slip (slip stitches purlwise with yarn in back unless indicated otherwise)
sl1yo	Bring yarn to front between needles, slip next stitch purlwise, bring yarn over needle and slipped stitch. If working a knit afterward, leave yarn in back ready to work a knit stitch; if working a purl afterward, bring yarn to front between needles ready to work a purl stitch
SM	Slip marker
ssk	Slip 2 stitches knitwise one at a time, knit them together through back loops
ssk cast-off	Ssk, *slip next stitch knitwise to right needle, insert left needle through front of both stitches on right needle, k2togtbl; rep from * as directed by pattern
ssp	Slip 2 stitches knitwise one at a time, slip stitches in new orientation back to left needle, purl stitches together through back loops
st(s)	Stitch(es)
St st	Stocking stitch (stockinette): Knit on RS rows, purl on WS rows
WS	Wrong side
wyib	With yarn held in back of work
wyif	With yarn held in front of work
yo	Yarn over needle and into working position

The following tutorials are available for techniques used in this book:

Long-tail cast-on
Pom Pom Issue 11 and *purlsoho.com/create/long-tail-cast-on*

Crochet provisional cast-on
Pom Pom Issue 15 and *vimeo.com/158459384*

Long-tail tubular cast-on
Pom Pom Issue 7

Tubular cast-off
Pom Pom Issue 7

Jeny's Surprisingly Stretchy cast-off
knitty.com/ISSUEfall09/FEATjssbo.php

Three-needle cast-off
Pom Pom issue 5 and *vimeo.com/171071650*

Kitchener stitch
Pom Pom issue 3 and *vimeo.com/158459385*

Acknowledgements

My knitting career has been a constant stream of grace and of others granting me trust that my vision is worth pursuing. This book is a shining example of others' faith in me and my work.

To the dyers and companies who graciously supplied yarn for the patterns in this book: thank you for trusting me with your art.

To John Arbon Textiles, who supplied the yarn for the swatches and examples in the Foundations chapter: thank you for your creative and joyful work in the yarn community.

To my sample knitters, Alison, Amy, Bonnie, Chaitanya, Chonita, Jessica, Minh, Rebecca and Darlene (my mom!): huge thanks for your perseverance, kindness, and ability to work to some impressive deadlines.

To my test knitters, Anoush, Belle, Carol, Catarina, Erendis of Numenor, Eva-Maria, Fie, Grace, Heather, Jacqui, Jaimie, Jen, Jessica, Leigh, Lynné, Sophie S, Sophie T, Steph, Stacy: thank you for your keen brains and quick fingers.

To my tech editors, Amelia and Emma: hoo boy. You took some pretty bonkers ideas and made them real, and I cannot thank you enough.

To the women of Pom Pom: your support, strength, and willingness to do the right thing without question astounds and overjoys me every time I work with you. I don't have enough words to say thank you.

To Emi Ito: thank you for your thoughtfulness and generosity in sharing your cultural perspective on origami and its place in art, Japanese history, and my work.

To those whose names grace the titles of these patterns: thank you for expanding the boundaries of your art forms and sharing them with the world, despite prejudices against your gender and ethnicity.

To every person who has told me their stories about *Knitting Outside the Box*, what it has meant for you and your knitting lives: thank you for believing in me and helping me know that I am doing this for a reason.

Finally, to my friends, to my parents, and to my little family of Will, George Michael, and Jashu: thank you for holding me close and loving me hard. The world is not wide enough to hold how much I love you and how much you mean to me.

About the Author

Bristol Ivy is a knitting designer and teacher from Portland, Maine. Her work focuses on the intersection of classic tailoring and innovative technique, and has been published by Quince & Co., Pom Pom Quarterly, Interweave Knits, amirisu, and many more. She is also the author of *Knitting Outside the Box*, published in 2017 by Pom Pom Press.

You can find her at **bristolivy.com** and on Twitter and Instagram as **@bristolivy**.